BUSINESS REPORTING:
HARNESSING THE POWER OF THE INTERNET FOR USERS

Vivien Beattie
Ken Pratt

University of Stirling

Published by
The Institute of Chartered Accountants of Scotland
Edinburgh

First Published 2001
The Institute of Chartered Accountants of Scotland

© 2001
ISBN 1 871250 90 0

Printed by Bell and Bain, Glasgow

Research Reports

Refereeing Process

The Research Committee applies a rigorous refereeing process to all stages of its research reports. The refereeing process operates by sending the initial research proposal to two independent referees (one academic and one practitioner). The academic referee will either be a member of the Panel listed below or an *ad hoc* referee. All proposals are also reviewed by the Director of Research who remains in close contact with the project. The two referees are consulted on the academic and technical standard of the draft research report. In particular, they are asked to comment on:

- the academic rigour of the document;

- the validity of the approach taken in the report;

- whether the presentation of the report identifies the key issues and brings these to the attention of the intended reader; and

- whether the document will add to the knowledge and understanding of the interested reader.

Professor N Garrod	University of Glasgow
Professor R H Gray	University of Glasgow
Professor J Haslam	Heriot-Watt University
Professor J Holland	University of Glasgow
Professor I Lapsley	University of Edinburgh
Professor T Lee	University of Alabama
Professor W M McInnes	University of Stirling
Professor S McLeay	University of Wales
Professor M J Page	University of Portsmouth
Professor C Roberts	University of Aberdeen
Professor M J Sherer	University of Essex
Professor R Taffler	Cranfield University
Professor P Walton	ESSEC, France
Professor P Weetman	University of Strathclyde
Professor R M S Wilson	University of Loughborough

The Research Committee is grateful to all those who participate in the refereeing process.

CONTENTS

FOREWORD

As its users know, the internet allows an enormous amount of information to be offered, and accessed, at very low cost. It thus creates a new and amazingly powerful opportunity to link together those who seek information and those who provide it.

In only a few years the power of these possibilities has stimulated the imagination of hundreds of millions of people and have resulted for many in a whole new way of communicating. Companies have recognised the benefits not only from vastly wider selling opportunities, but also from offering much improved communication opportunities to their stakeholders and others. Some of that communication has embraced corporate reporting.

However there is a snag. When communication is associated with personal interaction it is relatively easy to gauge people's reactions, and from this to judge what works and what does not. Yet merely offering on-line, data prepared for published hard copy purposes does nothing to harness the power of the medium. With internet based communication of complex issues, judging usage is hard and little direct feedback is usually available. And cost is important too, for although internet communications themselves are relatively cheap, preparing data specially for use on the net is not. So it is very difficult for providers of information to know what to provide. Even finding out what can be done and what others are doing is difficult and takes a great deal of time and the number of sources available on this issue alone can seem bewildering.

Yet at the end of the day, it is not what is offered that matters, but how well users needs are met. This research project is believed to be the first study of users' attitudes to web-based reporting. As a result it offers something unique and valuable to those who want to shape their reporting approach to what users want, coupled with the provision of a practical "feet on the ground" framework of issues to consider.

The Institute of Chartered Accountants of Scotland (ICAS) is proud of being the oldest accountancy body in the world. It is proud too of its tradition of ensuring that accounting practice does not stand still but continues to reflect the issues of the day. ICAS believes that web-based reporting is becoming a key tool for business reporting and commissioned this study to provide a perceptive snapshot of current and developing practice and the lessons already available. This research report summarises that study and we believe it will be of real use to those responsible for providing web-based corporate information and well as to a wider group of users, regulators and observers. We hope that you will agree!

Nigel Macdonald
Convener, Research Committee

December 2001

ACKNOWLEDGMENTS

The authors would like to thank the Research Committee of The Institute of Chartered Accountants of Scotland for funding this project. We also wish to thank Ann Lamb, Assistant Director, Research at ICAS for her help throughout the duration of the project and Isobel Webber for her care in typesetting the final report. The report has benefited from helpful comments from the reviewers, which were greatly appreciated.

Our thanks go also to those organisations and individuals who assisted us in compiling mailing lists (Stephen Fryer of UKSIP (formerly the Institute of Investment Management and Research), Brian Capon of the British Bankers' Association, Nick Stevens and Margot Owles of the UK Shareholders' Association, Jeremy King and Emma Rees of ProShare, the heads of audit in the largest accountancy firms and senior contacts in financial services companies). Most especially, however, we are indebted to the 538 individuals who gave so freely of their time in completing the questionnaire.

Finally, we would like to express our gratitude to Lesley Galloway (née Swan) who helped with the input of the questionnaire data and spent many of the days in the run-up to her marriage transcribing our interview tapes so carefully.

Executive Summary

Background

Use of the Internet to disseminate and access corporate information is growing rapidly and is being facilitated by regulatory changes. Preparers benefit from cost savings. Users can benefit in a variety of ways, depending on the extent to which the capabilities of the digital medium are exploited. Possibilities include enhanced timeliness, greater ease of access and search, and improved facilities for data extraction, automatic comparisons and analysis. In addition, the ability of the medium to handle the reporting of a greatly expanded information set fits well with recent calls for the increased disclosure of a broader range of information, including qualitative information, quantitative non-financial performance indicators, and forward-looking information.

Purpose of study and research approach

A discussion document published by the Research Committee of The Institute of Chartered Accountants of Scotland (ICAS, 1999) made seven proposals regarding business reporting, many of which directly involve the use of the web. The principal purpose of this study is to investigate the views held by interested parties regarding these proposals. A questionnaire was sent to 1,645 interested parties representing four primary groups involved with reporting by listed companies: expert users; private shareholders; finance directors; and audit partners. A total of 538 responses were received, giving an overall response rate of 33%. Sixteen follow-up telephone interviews were also conducted.

Secondary objectives of the study are: to ask general contextual questions regarding the reporting obligations of listed companies and those having a right to be consulted on issues to do with business reporting; and to explore specific issues to emerge from the wider debate on web-based reporting.

This study represents, to the best of our knowledge, the first study of users' attitudes to web-based reporting, thereby complementing the many studies of web-reporting practices. A major feature of the study is that it allows the views and attitudes of the main interest groups in business reporting to be systematically *compared*, so that points of general agreement and points of major disagreement can be identified. Evidence of this type is of particular value to standard setters, whose role it is to encourage best practice and to consider (and, if appropriate, attempt to reduce or resolve) conflicts of interest between different groups.

The questionnaire also covered content and assurance aspects of business reporting, and two separate reports will present these findings.

Key findings

In this summary of key findings, descriptive labels, rather than numbers, are used to present the questionnaire results. Levels of agreement are described as 'strong', 'reasonably strong' or 'mild'. The extent of usefulness is described as 'extremely useful', 'useful' or 'moderately useful'. An explanation of the precise meaning of these labels can be found towards the end of chapter one.

Company reporting obligations

- **Extent of listed company's reporting obligations to various stakeholder groups**

  There is a very high level of consensus across the respondent groups regarding the reporting obligations that a listed company has in relation to various stakeholder groups. Existing investors are given top priority, with 84% of the respondents rating the obligation to them as 'absolute'. Potential investors and employees also rank highly, with 73% of the respondents rating the obligation to potential investors as 'major' or 'absolute', while the figure for employees is 63%. Employees were rated highly because of the importance of intellectual capital to many businesses. The other three groups (community/public, suppliers and customers) rate less highly, but nevertheless significantly.

- **Need to consult private shareholders on external reporting issues**

  On average, private shareholders agreed strongly that private shareholders should be consulted on external reporting issues whereas the level of agreement of other respondent groups was mild.

Attitudes to ICAS (1999) proposals re web reporting

- **Requirement to disclose key information**

  On average, both user groups are reasonably strongly in agreement that management should make key management information available (subject to legitimate concerns), while finance directors are mildly against this and audit partners are neutral. There is a high level of dispersion of views within groups.

- **Requirement to layer information**

  All groups, on average, agree that it is desirable to layer information to avoid information overload. The level of dispersion within groups is generally very low.

- **Requirement to maintain free search facility**

  Users were, on average, most strongly in favour of this requirement, exhibiting reasonably strong support. Finance directors were, as a group, neutral, though they exhibited the highest degree of dispersion (moderate), with audit partners' views falling, on average, between those of users and finance directors.

- **Requirement to provide pre-packaged information**

  Although, on average, both user groups (especially private shareholders) favour this idea, support is only 'mild' for expert users. Finance directors and audit partners are, on average, neutral. The level of dispersion in views varies from low for expert users to high for audit partners.

- **Requirement to place records of general meetings on web**

  On average, three groups strongly agree, exhibiting a very low level of dispersion in views. Finance directors agree only mildly, and display a high level of dispersion in their views.

- **Requirement to place audio-visual record of general meetings on web**

  Both user groups offer reasonably strong support for this, with audit partners giving mild support and finance directors being neutral. The level of dispersion varies from high for finance directors to low for audit partners.

- **Requirement to broadcast general meetings with financial analysts/institutional shareholders**

  Perhaps surprisingly, there is no general support from *any* group for webcasting (or broadcasting *via* satellite television) these meetings – both user groups are, on average, neutral while finance directors and audit partners are against (audit partners mildly and finance directors reasonably strongly). The level of dispersion ranges from moderate for expert users to very low for audit partners.

- **Requirement to place minutes of one-to-one meetings on web**

  There are extreme differences between the views of the four groups. The two user groups are, unusually, very divided. On average, expert users are mildly against the proposal while private shareholders are mildly in favour, although the dispersion in views is at least high in both cases. Although audit partners are, on average, neutral, finance directors are strongly opposed, with low dispersion.

- **Requirement to webcast AGM**

  Both user groups, on average, gave reasonably strong support for this proposal, with audit partners offering mild support. Finance directors mildly opposed the proposal. The level of dispersion of views within groups was generally low (the exception being the finance director group).

- **Requirement to replace AGM with online questioning**

  All groups, on average, rejected this proposal. With the exception of private shareholders, the level of rejection was mild, but private shareholders expressed reasonably strong disagreement. For all four groups, however, the level of dispersion was moderate or high.

- **Requirement to update website information periodically, not continuously**

  On average, all groups agree (either mildly or reasonably strongly) that more frequent, periodic updating is preferable, with no significant differences between the groups. Audit partners, who most strongly support this proposal, display very low dispersion, with two-thirds responding 'agree'.

- **Requirement to disclose frequency of updating**

  Finance directors' support for this proposal was, on average, reasonably strong, with strong support from the other three groups. There was also very low dispersion in the views of each group.

Related observations

Taking these findings as a whole, several further observations can be made:

- There is a reasonably high general level of support for three proposals (place records of general meetings on the web; disclose the frequency of updating; and layer information).
- By contrast, there is little general support for three other proposals (place minutes of one-to-one meetings on the web; broadcast general meetings; and replace the AGM with online questioning).
- The views held by the respondent groups differ significantly for all proposals but one (update website information periodically, not continuously). Preparers, in particular, support very few of the proposals, yet both user groups agree (often quite strongly) with the majority of the proposals, while auditors' views tend to fall in between. There are clearly conflicts of interest present.
- The views of expert users and private shareholders are very similar.
- The level of within-group dispersion of views is consistently high in relation to only one proposal (requirement to disclose key information). This indicates the general lack of consensus in relation to this critical issue.
- Respondents who were more familiar with the Internet (*ie* more frequent users) expressed a stronger level of agreement with six proposals involving the extended use of the Internet for business reporting.
- During interviews, respondents identified a range of advantages and disadvantages in relation to each of the proposals.

Usefulness of navigation aids, search aids and file formats

- **Index business reporting information on home page**

  The groups display very similar responses to this feature, with all groups rating the feature, on average, approximately mid-way between 'useful' and 'very useful'. This is the feature ranked by all groups as most useful out of all those considered. Dispersion was very low for all groups.

- **Hyperlinked site map or table of contents available**

  All groups rank this feature as either the second or third most useful. Dispersion was very low for all groups.

- **Hyperlinks**

  Of the six types of link considered, both user groups and finance directors, on average, rank the link between the financial statements and the relevant note to the accounts and the link between the financial statements and the relevant section of the OFR first and second, respectively. Audit partners reverse these rankings. There are, however, significant differences between the four groups' perceived level of usefulness of hyperlinks, with users and auditors rating them more highly than preparers. The least useful link according to users and finance directors is that between the OFR and relevant company background. The level of within-group dispersion was generally low or very low, although finance directors and audit partners had more varied views regarding the usefulness of the link between the financial statements and the five-year summary (moderate dispersion).

- **Ability to create graphs of data series**

  Users (especially the private shareholder group) rate this feature significantly more highly that the other groups (especially finance directors) – the mean response for both user groups is within the 'useful' range, while those of finance directors and audit partners fall within the 'moderately useful' range. Within-group dispersion was either low or very low.

- **Next and previous buttons**

  All four groups, on average, rank this feature as useful (borderline extremely useful). Within-group dispersion was in all cases very low.

- **Email alerts**

  All four groups, on average, rank this feature as useful (borderline extremely useful). Within-group dispersion was in all cases very low.

- **File formats**

  The 'don't know' category is quite large for many of these questions, especially for users and for the XBRL format. If the responses of all groups are combined, the spreadsheet format is seen as being of most use, followed by word-processed files and the XBRL format. The more common current formats (HTML and PDF) trail slightly behind in the rankings. Expert users and audit partners appear to rate type tags that allow automatic comparisons more highly than the other two groups.

  There are, however, distinct differences in the rankings of the groups. Expert users rank the spreadsheet format top and HTML last. Private shareholders, by contrast, rank HTML top. Finance directors do not appear to make a significant distinction between the five formats, while audit partners rate PDF significantly below the rest. The level of within-group dispersion was very variable, reflecting the groups' varying levels of familiarity with the different formats. Private shareholders displayed either moderate or high dispersion for the five formats; at the other extreme, audit partners displayed either low or very low dispersion.

Related observations

Taking these findings as a whole, several further observations can be made:

- All of the features are considered by all respondent groups to be, on average, at least fairly useful (mean < 3.0).
- In general, the three features considered to be most useful were: index business reporting information on home page; hyperlinked site map or table of contents available; and hyperlinks between financial statements and notes.
- In general, the four features considered to be least useful were the availability of alternative file formats: word-processed; XBRL; HTML; and PDF.
- The views of the four groups were significantly different for about half of the features (four types of hyperlink; ability to create graphs of data series; four of the file formats and type tags). Preparers tended to rate the usefulness of features to users below the usefulness rating given by users themselves.
- Respondents who were more familiar with the Internet perceived four features to have a greater level of usefulness than those with less familiarity.
- During interviews, respondents identified a number of advantages and disadvantages in relation to some of the features.

Recommendations

Based on these findings, eight recommendations are made. These recommendations are based not only on the average level of desirability/usefulness of the proposal/feature, but also on the degree of both *across*-group consensus and *within*-group consensus. A lack of *across*-group consensus indicates the existence of a conflict of interests between groups, based on their evaluation of the costs and benefits of the proposal/feature to their group. A lack of *within*-group consensus suggests the existence of uncertainty regarding the true identity and magnitude of costs and benefits to a specific group that shares a common interest (or a lack of homogeneity within the group).

Company reporting obligations

Recommendation 1: Corporate reporting practices should be developed (through the joint efforts of regulators, companies, the accountancy profession and academics) to satisfy the specialist information needs of stakeholder groups other than existing shareholders. In particular, the needs of potential investors and employees should be addressed, where the majority of respondents view the obligation to report as either 'major' or 'absolute'.

> *Justification*: All interested parties appear to accept that other stakeholder groups are legitimate user groups, to whom listed companies owe a reporting obligation.

Recommendation 2: Private shareholders should be consulted by those with a role in the development of corporate reporting practices (*i.e.* regulators, companies, the accountancy profession and academics) on issues related to company external reporting. (Note that the other recommendations in this report accord equal status to the expressed views of private shareholders.)

> *Justification*: All interested parties (especially private shareholders) expressed this view. It is widely recognised that users are not well represented in the policy-making process (for example, there is a general absence of written submissions by users to rule-making bodies). It is likely, therefore, that the views of user groups will have to be actively sought out.

Attitudes to ICAS (1999) proposals re web-reporting

Recommendation 3: Policy makers should consider requiring (or at least encouraging *via* best practice guidelines) the following five ICAS (1999) proposals:

- place records of general meetings on web
- disclose frequency of web updating
- layer information
- maintain free search facility
- place audio-visual record of general meetings on web.

> *Justification*: On average, both user groups support these proposals strongly or reasonably strongly and preparers are at worst neutral. It seems clear, therefore, that the advantages of these proposals outweigh the disadvantages.

Recommendation 4: There should be no immediate moves made to encourage or require the following three ICAS (1999) proposals:

- place minutes of one-to-one meetings on web
- broadcast general meetings
- replace AGM with online questioning.

   Justification: On average, *all* groups either disagree or are neutral towards these proposals (the minor exception is that private shareholders mildly agree that the minutes of one-to-one meetings be placed on the web). It seems clear, therefore, that the perceived disadvantages of these proposals currently outweigh the advantages.

Recommendation 5: Further research should be conducted to investigate the nature, magnitude and incidence of the costs and benefits relating to two ICAS (1999) proposals:

- disclose key information
- webcast AGM.

   Justification: On average, these proposals receive reasonably strong support from both user groups, yet preparers are in mild disagreement. Thus, these changes are unlikely to be instigated by preparers and would require regulation. It is, therefore, critical that the costs and benefits are well understood before there is regulatory intervention. In particular, many commentators argue that the disclosure of key information used to manage the company is essential to the development of business reporting. Unfortunately, there are perceived to be major potential disadvantages to be set against the major potential advantages (in particular, the issue of commercial confidentiality). To what extent are expressed concerns about commercial confidentiality excuses, genuinely perceived threats (yet without significant substance) or actual threats?

Recommendation 6: Further research is desirable to investigate the nature, magnitude and incidence of the costs and benefits relating to two ICAS (1999) proposals:

- update website periodically, not continuously
- provide pre-packaged information.

   Justification: On average, these proposals receive only mild support from both user groups (the exception is that private shareholders agree reasonably strongly that pre-packaged information be provided), and preparers are also mildly supportive or neutral. Thus, these proposals are perceived to have some potential advantages and no major disadvantages.

Usefulness of navigation aids, search aids and file formats

Recommendation 7: Best practice guidelines should be introduced by those with a role in the development of corporate reporting practices (*i.e.* regulators, companies, the accountancy profession and academics) to encourage preparers to incorporate the following navigation and search aids into their websites:

- index of business reporting information on home page
- hyperlinked site map or table of contents
- hyperlinks between
  - financial statements and notes
  - financial statements and OFR
  - financial statements and five-year summary
  - notes and OFR
  - OFR and forward-looking information
- point and click graph facility
- next and previous buttons
- email alerts
- type tags to facilitate automatic comparisons.

Justification: Preparers are shown (in the absence of any concerns regarding the potential disadvantages of the features) to systematically *underestimate* the perceived usefulness of most features to users. On average, both user groups rate these features as either extremely useful or useful, while preparers and auditors rate them at least moderately useful. The likely advantages to users are, therefore, significant but, in the absence of some intervention, underprovision seems likely to occur.

Recommendation 8: Research should be conducted to investigate the validity of concerns that the provision of alternative file formats that can be manipulated will have adverse consequences.

Justification: The potential benefits of these formats are considerable in terms of the speed and ease of data transfer and analysis; however the risks associated with accidental corruption, tampering and bias demand careful consideration.

General conclusion

An important general conclusion to emerge from this study is that there is widespread support for changes that either widen access to information (by supplementing existing communication channels with web reporting) or increase the ease of access (by utilising the technical features of the web medium). There is, however, some caution expressed where it is feared that supplementary web communications may impair the information quality of existing people-based disclosures. Respondents appear to reject the idea of *substituting* people-based communication with web-based communication.

CHAPTER ONE

INTRODUCTION

This introductory chapter presents the background to the study, by considering briefly the impact that the Internet is having on corporate reporting and outlining the proposals made by ICAS (1999) and others regarding the electronic delivery and dissemination of business reporting information. The purpose of the study and the research approach adopted is then set out. The final section outlines the structure of the report.

Background

This section considers trends in Internet use, regulatory changes relating to the use of the Internet for corporate reporting (*i.e.* web-based, Internet or digital reporting), the advantages of web-based reporting, and the implications of changes in the business environment for the traditional reporting model.

Trends in Internet use

Throughout the developed world, there has been a substantial increase in access to the Internet in recent years. For example, *Newsnight* reported that 30% of UK households now have access to the Internet (14 November 2000), while a survey by the Office for National Statistics reported in September 2000 that 45% of adults in Britain have accessed the Internet at some time.

Use of the Internet to access corporate information is also growing. A major telephone survey of 1000 private shareholders (weighted to reflect the demographic characteristics of the national population) was undertaken for ProShare in 1999 (ProShare, 1999). It was found that 7% expressed a current preference for receiving information *via* the Internet, 25% said they would in the future consider using the Internet, and 16% used the Internet as an information source when buying shares. A global study undertaken in 1996 reported that investors ranked websites a lowly fourth from bottom out of 23 possible sources of information. Only two years later, this information source had risen to 13th out of 26 sources (Taylor, 1998).

A consequence of this is that many commentators are predicting that the printed annual report will gradually disappear as corporate reports increasingly move to the worldwide electronic medium of the Internet (*e.g.* Bury, 1999; Nordberg, 1999; Romain, 2000). On the supply side, Deller *et al.* (1999) examined the use of the Internet to provide financial information by the top 100 companies in the US, UK and Germany. They found that over 90% of US companies provide extensive financial information, with UK and German companies also providing a considerable amount of information, although they lagged behind the US.

Regulatory changes

The shift towards web-based reporting could not occur without significant legal reform. The UK government launched a major review of company law in March 1998 (DTI, 1998). In February 1999, a consultation document was issued by the Company Law Review Steering Group (DTI, 1999a). This document indicates a willingness to introduce any legal changes necessary to facilitate desirable changes in company reporting, including those attributable to changes in information and communications technology. Following a second major Consultation Document (DTI, 2000a) in March 2000, the Steering Group published a third later in the same year. This proposes that, for listed companies, both preliminary announcements and full annual reports be published on a website, with electronic notification of that fact to shareholders that register for this (DTI, 2000b, pp116-7). A final report, containing essentially similar recommendations, was issued in July 2001 (DTI, 2001, p196).

Internet reporting has been given further impetus by the Companies Act 1985 (Electronic Communications) Order 2000, enacted in December 2000. This allows companies to meet their statutory reporting obligations to shareholders either by distributing annual financial reports electronically or by posting them on the company website and advising shareholders that this has been done[1].

Advantages of Internet reporting

Both companies and users see advantages in the use of the Internet to disseminate financial information. Not least for companies, there can be cost benefits. The Investor Relations Society in the UK (1998) estimated that it cost between £20,000 and £30,000 per annum to maintain financial information on a website, while by comparison it cost, on average, £5 to send out a copy of the annual report. Thus, web costs are quickly recouped. In addition, the company can both broaden and segment its disclosure audience (Ashbaugh *et al.* 1999, p248).

For users, the potential advantages lie in the ease of access and ease of search (Thompson, 1996). Sophisticated, user-friendly software agents provide the user with effective decision-support facilities. Information can be made available more quickly, potentially on a real-time basis. Moreover, use of the Internet means that there is no longer any significant technological or cost constraint on the amount of information that can be disseminated.

Changes in the business environment and implications for the reporting model

These characteristics of Internet reporting mesh well with broader changes occurring in the business environment; in particular, the shift towards consumer-driven business and the increasing importance of 'soft' assets such as intellectual capital. (For a review of changes in the business environment, see ICAS (1999, pp6-7).) These changes, combined with users' increasing demands for greater transparency from companies, have led organisations in many countries to question the continued adequacy of the traditional historical financial reporting model to user needs[2]. This has raised the prospect of potentially fundamental changes in business reporting, involving the disclosure of a much greater volume of information, especially forward-looking, non-financial and qualitative information (see Beattie (2000) for a review). This increase in content is greatly facilitated by the new methods of dissemination.

Business Reporting: The Inevitable Change? (ICAS, 1999)

In February 1999, the Research Committee of The Institute of Chartered Accountants of Scotland (ICAS) published a discussion document setting out its view of 'inevitable changes' in business reporting (ICAS, 1999, pp68-78). This view is based upon a survey of users, preparers and auditors which investigated attitudes towards four themes: the cyclical nature of corporate communication; differential user access to company information; information overload; and the need for confidence in business information.

Based on the survey findings, seven proposals were made regarding the means of dissemination, the structure and content of the information provided, and the nature of related assurance services. Five of the proposals directly involve the use of electronic delivery and dissemination. Specifically, it proposed that:

- Large sections of the corporate database be made available to external users electronically. This addresses users' general desire for additional information available on an as-demanded basis.

- Information within the database be layered, with links to external information sources and a facility for free search. The layering feature addresses the information overload concerns of some non-expert users, while providing for the detailed information desired by other users. This feature also facilitates effective search strategies. The free search principle satisfies the desire of users to retain, at their option, control over the search and selection process.

- Information be available in pre-packaged forms based on templates relevant to each stakeholder group. This addresses the needs of non-expert users who can opt to simply access the relevant template, drilling down to whatever level of detail they specify; it also provides the relevant focus suited to different stakeholder perspectives.

- Access to general company meetings be extended *via* live broadcast; records and minutes of both general and one-to-one meetings being accessible electronically; a facility for on-line questioning of management being made available[3]. The extension of access reduces the unfair advantage aspect of corporate communications while retaining the benefits of company meetings; it also facilitates the subjective assessment of 'quality of management', which was ranked as the most important generic factor driving company performance. On-line questioning allows interaction which, among other things, enhances corporate governance.

- The database be updated more quickly and frequently. This overcomes users' expressed moderate dissatisfaction with the timeliness of corporate reporting while retaining the perceived advantages of regular, periodic information flows.

Purpose of study and research approach

The principal purpose of this study is to investigate the views held by interested parties regarding the ICAS (1999) proposals. To do this, a questionnaire was sent to 1,645 interested parties representing four primary groups involved with reporting by listed companies: expert users; private shareholders; finance directors; and audit partners[4]. Sixteen follow-up telephone interviews were also conducted (7 with expert users, 2 with private shareholders, 3 with finance directors and 4 with audit partners).

In addition to asking specific questions about the ICAS (1999) proposals, this study also took the opportunity to explore related specific issues to emerge from the wider debate. These were identified from a comprehensive review of the professional and academic literature on changes in business reporting published up to mid-2000. As a consequence, the questionnaire was both wide ranging and detailed, and findings are, therefore, written up in three separate reports. This report focuses on web-reporting issues (*i.e.* the delivery and structure of the business reporting package); separate reports will address content and assurance[5].

This study represents, to the best of our knowledge, the first study of users' attitudes to web-based reporting. This complements the many studies of web-reporting practices. A major feature of the study is that it allows the views and attitudes of the main interest groups in business reporting to be systematically compared, so that points of general agreement and points of major disagreement can be identified. Formal statistical tests are performed to determine whether observed group differences are statistically significant. Descriptive evidence of this type is of particular value to standard setters, whose role it is to encourage best practice and to consider (and, if appropriate, attempt to reduce or resolve) conflicts of interest between different groups. These conflicts generally arise from the different incentives, motivations and experiences of the groups. Small, private shareholders tend to have quite different incentives and experiences from institutional shareholders and other professional users. They were, therefore, surveyed as a separate group.

Questions asked

This report covers four main questions dealing with the Internet. The first question asked about the frequency with which the respondent used the Internet. This reveals whether the views held are associated with Internet familiarity, as might be expected. The second question focused on the ICAS (1999) proposals discussed earlier, some of which echo those suggested by others. Respondents were asked to indicate the extent to which they agreed or disagreed with the proposals, on a five-point scale ranging from 1 (strongly agree) to 5 (strongly disagree).

The third question dealt with various navigation and search aids, with subsidiary questions based on the features of the *FauxCom* project (FASB, 1998) and FASB (2000) – see chapter two for a discussion of these studies. The fourth and final question dealt with file formats, and was based on FASB (2000). The latter two questions asked about the usefulness of the various features and formats and elicited responses on a five-point scale of 1 (very useful) to 5 (not useful at all).

In all questions, a 'don't know' response category was included. This was considered particularly important for the Internet-related questions since a significant number of respondents might be wholly unfamiliar with the Internet and, therefore, feel unable to answer the questions.

This first report also reports on two general, scene-setting, contextual questions that were asked of respondents. The first concerned the extent of listed companies' reporting obligations to various stakeholder groups. The second asked about the extent to which private shareholders should be consulted on issues related to the nature of corporate reporting.

The section of the questionnaire covered by this report is reproduced in the Appendix.

Respondent groups and response rates

Expert users included investment analysts (members of UKSIP, the UK Society of Investment Professionals), fund managers (employed by leading firms) and corporate lenders (employed by banks engaged in corporate lending). Private shareholders were approached with the assistance of the UK Shareholders' Association (UKSA) and ProShare. Listed company finance directors were identified using commercial databases. Finally, listed company audit partners were approached with the assistance of the heads of audit in 12 of the top 20 UK audit firms.

Of the 1,645 questionnaires sent out (with two follow ups), 538 responses were received. This represents a response rate of 33%, which compares very favourably with the rates obtained by recent surveys of the same or similar populations. A detailed breakdown of the number of questionnaires issued and replies received is given in Table 1.1.

Table 1.1 Respondent groups and response rates

Group	No. in sample	No. responding	Response rate %
Expert users	588	159	27
Non-expert users: private shareholders	543	235	43
Preparers: finance directors	421	83	20
Auditors: audit partners	93	61	66
Total	**1645**	**538**	**33**

Presentation and display of results

Results for each question are presented mainly using graphic displays with supporting summary data. As the responses are limited to six categories (including 'don't know'), the frequency distribution of responses for each respondent group can effectively be shown graphically by means of a 100% divided bar chart. Where any of the categories represents 1% or less of total responses, it is excluded from the graphic display to aid clarity. For this reason, percentages may not add to 100%. The mean (average) and standard deviation provide additional useful summary data about the distribution of responses.

The standard deviation (SD) is a formal measure of the dispersion of responses and therefore indicates the level of consensus within a group. For example, given a five-point response scale of 1 to 5, the standard deviation is 0 if everyone responds '3' and 2 if half of the group responds '1' and the other half responds '5'. In practice, the standard deviations observed tend to fall between 0.5 and 1.5. Rather than reporting the actual numbers, descriptive labels have been used to indicate the level of dispersion as follows: very low ($SD \leq 0.9$); low ($0.9 \, SD \leq 1.0$); moderate ($1.0 \leq SD < 1.1$); high ($1.1 \leq SD < 1.2$); very high ($SD > 1.2$).

In some cases, the reporting of results is limited to the summary measures (using a column graph to display mean responses). In other cases, a table is used to present the key summary data.

For each question, a statistical test is performed to determine whether the observed difference between the four respondent groups is statistically significant[6].

Where the agree-disagree scale is used (mainly chapter four), the commentary accompanying the results sometimes refers to the combined 'strongly agree' and 'agree' categories as a 'positive' view, and the combined 'strongly disagree' and 'disagree' categories as a 'negative' view.

The actual verbal anchors used in the questionnaire were, for the agree-disagree scale, 1 = 'strongly agree'; 2 = 'agree'; 3 = 'neutral'; 4 = 'disagree'; and 5 = 'strongly disagree'. For the usefulness scale they were 1 = 'very useful'; 2 = 'useful'; 3 = 'fairly useful'; 4 = 'of little use'; and 5 = 'not useful at all'. Because the mean responses are more tightly clustered than the response scales, alternative descriptive labels facilitate the discussion of results. For the agree-disagree scale, the following descriptive labels are used:

Mean response	Descriptive label
<2.0	Strong agreement
2.0 to 2.5	Reasonably strong agreement
2.5 to 2.8	Mild agreement
2.8 to 3.2	Neutral
3.2 to 3.5	Mild disagreement
3.5 to 3.8	Reasonably strong disagreement
>3.8	Strong disagreement

For the usefulness scale (mainly chapter five), the range of mean group responses lies between 1.44 and 2.68 for the questions in chapter five and the following descriptive labels reflect this observed range:

Mean response	Descriptive label
1.4 to 1.7	Extremely useful
1.7 to 2.3	Useful
2.3 to 2.68	Moderately useful

Structure of the report

Chapter two begins by considering the new accountabilities of public companies. It proceeds to provide a review of the professional and academic literature relating to web-based reporting. This includes both discursive and empirical literature from around the world. While many empirical studies have documented the web practices of companies, the present study appears to be the first to ask users about their attitudes and preferences in relation to Internet reporting.

Chapters three to six present the results of the survey. Chapter three reports on the general, scene-setting questions about company reporting obligations and views regarding private shareholder consultation. Chapter four covers views on the ICAS (1999) proposals, while chapter five considers the usefulness of navigation aids, search aids and file formats. Whereas chapters four and five consider each issue separately, chapter six compares the groups across the entire set of questions, to provide a more holistic view of each group 'profile' and how the groups differ from each other.

Chapter seven presents conclusions and recommendations.

Endnotes:

[1] The APB (2001) Bulletin offers guidance to auditors in relation to web-based reporting. Auditors should review the process of electronic publication, check that the contents of the electronic version are identical to the hard copy, and check that there is no distortion in overall presentation. If not satisfied, auditors should refuse to give consent to the electronic release of their audit opinion. The wording of the auditors' report should be altered to refer to the financial statements by name rather than by page number.

[2] Although some commentators talk about the continued 'relevance' of the traditional accounting model, most would agree that the traditional model is necessary, but no longer sufficient, to meet the needs of users.

[3] ICAS (1999, p74) suggests that the two principal functions of the Annual General Meeting (AGM), the opportunity for questioning of management by shareholders and voting, could be conducted more effectively via the Internet.

[4] The expert user group was further split into three distinct sub-groups – investment analysts, *i.e.* sell-side analysts, fund managers, *i.e.* buy-side analysts and corporate lenders. However, as the analysis showed very few significant differences between the three expert groups, results for these groups are not provided separately.

[5] To the extent that changes in content are dependent upon the Internet for feasibility reasons (*e.g.* making minutes of general company meetings publicly available), they are considered in this report.

[6] Specifically, a parametric analysis of variance (ANOVA) is conducted, using a 5% significance level. The non-parametric Kruskal-Wallis one-way ANOVA by ranks test, which is arguably more appropriate given the nature of the data, gave equivalent significance levels to the parametric ANOVA in virtually all cases.

CHAPTER TWO

LITERATURE REVIEW

This chapter begins by considering briefly the expanding reporting obligations of companies. It then outlines representative views regarding the impact of technology on business reporting. Prototype web-based business reporting packages, which incorporate the unique, desirable features of the medium for corporate communication, are then discussed. This is followed by a discussion of the various Internet reporting formats, including an explanation of XBRL and its implications. The findings of recent surveys of company web reporting are then reviewed. Finally, the policy maker's dilemma in the face of conflicts of interest between interested parties is discussed.

Company reporting obligations

Corporate accountabilities are influenced by social, economic and political factors and so are subject to change. 'Accountability' can be defined as a process activated by an obligation: one party owes a timely reckoning to another about some past or future action and fulfills the obligation. Companies have many accountabilities, because they have many stakeholders: investors; suppliers; employees; customers; the government; and society at large. Elliott (1994, pp114-5) argues that information technology makes it easier to discharge accountability obligations because it is easier to record, report and transmit data, and concludes that existing accountabilities will be transformed.

In recent years, greater emphasis has been given to the needs of stakeholders other than shareholders. (A 'stakeholder' is defined as 'any group or individual who can affect or is affected by the achievement of the organisation's objectives' (Freeman, 1984, p46)). Stakeholder theory is based upon the twin premises that companies are accountable to all their stakeholders and that a major objective of management is to balance the conflicting demands of the various stakeholder groups (Ansoff, 1987, p51).

This stakeholder view has permeated through to the debate on business reporting. The RSA Inquiry envisioned a more inclusive approach to both business practices and business reporting. It recommended that the annual report be split into a single core document, published and available on the Internet, supplemented by reports aimed at specific stakeholder groups (RSA, 1995; 1998). (For a more detailed discussion, see ICAS (1999, pp17-18).) More recently, the 'inclusive' approach to business conduct has been debated during the company law review (DTI, 2000a, p*viii*).

Impact of technology on business reporting

In recent years, many influential individuals and organisations have considered the impact of developments in information and communications technology on business reporting. For example, the chairman of the American Institute of Certified Public Accountants (AICPA) Special Committee on Assurance Services, Robert Elliott (1992) argued that information technology is changing everything – it is changing profoundly the way that business is done and that this requires changes in external accounting. He called for greater disclosure of non-financial information, more frequent reporting and less aggregated reporting (pp74-75). Elliott (1994, p111) argued that companies could define 'views' into its database for different user groups.

Similarly, Wallman, a former US Securities and Exchange Commissioner, was among the first to identify the implications of new technologies for corporate reporting. He argued that there should be additional reporting of soft assets and of business risks, more frequent reporting, and disaggregated reporting *via* online access to sections of the company's management information system (1995). He proposed a disaggregated, user-controlled 'access' model (1997), pointing out that, due to the low cost of information dissemination and the existence of intelligent agents (sophisticated software), there was no longer any rationale for preparers to aggregate information. Users could then use the disaggregated information as inputs to their own customised analytical models.

Prototype web-based packages

Issues relating to the structure and nature of a web-based report were addressed in the *FauxCom* project of the Financial Accounting Standards Board (FASB) (1998). FASB launched FauxCom as a sample business information reporting package on its website that responds to and illustrates the information needs of investors and creditors as understood by the AICPA Special Committee on Financial Reporting (The Jenkins Report, AICPA, 1994).

This fully-integrated web-based package has been specifically designed to exploit the search, selection and analysis capabilities of modern technology. The package allows drilling down to the desired level of detail and provides navigation buttons which allow the user to jump between the financial statements, the related notes, five-year summaries, and the Management Discussion and Analysis (MDA). Graphs are available at the press of a button and information can be downloaded directly to Excel files.

In a similar vein, the ICAEW (1998) launched an interactive, prototype annual report, structured as a core report with supplementary reports, at a one-day conference on *The 21st Century Annual Report.*

Internet reporting formats: PDF, HTML and XBRL

The Internet offers enormous potential advantages to the global business information supply chain. Currently, the two most popular methods of Internet reporting are *Adobe Acrobat*™ (PDF) and HTML. Due to the disadvantages of each of these, a new method XBRL, is being developed to provide 'a common transport language to facilitate the exchange and the dissemination of financial data online' (McClausland, 2000).

PDF

Adobe Inc. developed the popular *Adobe Acrobat*™ program for Internet publishing. The files produced by this program are known as PDF (portable document format) files, because they preserve all formatting in a document, regardless of the platform application used to read it. Thus, it creates documents that are identical to the original printed document both when viewed on screen and when printed. The format is widely accessible, since the Acrobat Reader (a special plug-in) can be downloaded freely from the web.

The format also provides document security, as the creator of the file can set the document such that those who read the document are unable to copy or modify the text or graphics[7]. Of course, this is also a limitation, as users can only view documents – they cannot extract data or modify the documents to undertake further analysis. Annual report files are typically very large and, therefore, slow to download. PDF allows hyperlinking *out of* but not *into* specific places within the file.

HTML

HTML was first developed for text-based documents. Its popularity as an Internet language arose from the introduction of visual/graphic web browsers (Internet Explorer and Netscape Communicator are currently the two most popular web browsers). HTML specifies a set of structural and semantic tags to describe how elements are to appear on a page (*e.g.* tags relating to some formatting and the use of hyperlinks and multimedia). Documents can be viewed directly in the browser and HTML readily supports hyperlinking.

However HTML does not specify in detail how documents are to be presented. Consequently the printed document can look quite different from the original, which is a major limitation.

XBRL

The advantages of electronic financial information are likely to be greatly enhanced by the development of XBRL, which stands for eXtensible Business Reporting Language. It uses XML (eXtensible mark-up language - the next generation from HTML) to create documents where specific pieces of information are 'tagged' in plain language. This allows for easy exchange of information between formats. XML users can either create their own tags or use those created by others to describe document content (semantic meaning). Importantly, the tags separate semantic content from document presentation. New tags can be added as required, *i.e.* the language is 'extensible', which increases its usability.

XBRL is the XML standard for the financial reporting 'industry'. It is a classification scheme that lists all of the data elements that the XBRL Committee deems relevant and specifies how each element relates to others. For each data element, the taxonomy specifies:

- a unique identifier;
- the commonly used English name (element label);
- the immediate parent;
- the mathematical relationship between child and parent item (*i.e.* addition, subtraction or no relationship);
- a description;
- a customary order in which the item is presented in a financial statement; and
- the authority that indicates why the item is included in the taxonomy.

The taxonomy will be modified to suit each separate jurisdiction. A draft of the taxonomy based on IAS GAAP has recently been published (see http://www.xbrl.org/core/2000-07-31/metamodel.xsd) .

The AICPA, in conjunction with others such as the International Accounting Standards Board (IASB), has set up a working party to develop a version of XML for corporate reporting. Every element of the financial statements, and Operating and Financial Review (OFR), will be coded using a simple tag. This technology supports tailor-made extraction of data and comparison across companies (XBRL, 2000). The technology would be freely licensed, to encourage adoption by annual report preparers and their auditors. The major software sellers have committed to developing software (automatic extraction tools) that will incorporate XBRL into their financial packages.

The advantages of XBRL are that information would be keyed in only once. With the click of a mouse, users would be able to automatically extract information from the Internet and transfer it to, say, Excel for comparison and further analysis.

Surveys of company practice

Over recent years, several studies have documented companies' growing use of their websites for business reporting purposes in addition to promotional and sales material. Many are single-country studies:

- US – Petravick and Gillett (1998); Louwers *et al.* (1996) and FASB (2000);
- UK – Hussey *et al.* (1998); Marston and Leow (1998); Hussey and Sowinska (1999); Craven and Marston (1999); Financial Director (2000);
- Ireland – Brennan and Hourigan (2000);
- Spain – Gowthorpe and Amat (1999);
- Sweden – Hedlin (1999); and
- Austria – Pirchegger and Wagenhofer (1999).

Others involve a comparison of several countries: Lymer and Tallberg (1997) consider the UK and Finland; Deller *et al.* consider the US, the UK and Germany. Yet others are worldwide: Taylor (1998), IASC (1999) and PricewaterhouseCoopers (2000).

A summary of many of these studies can be found in IASC (1999, pp44-46) and FASB (2000, pp33-35) and so only the most recent and wide-ranging studies are considered here. These studies generally document four things: the existence of corporate websites; the frequency with which any financial information is included therein; the type of financial information included; and features of the website, in particular navigation and search aids and downloads.

US

As part of its Business Reporting Research Project, FASB has undertaken a study into the electronic distribution of business reporting information (FASB, 2000). This study examines in great detail the Internet reporting practices of the Fortune 100 companies as at 30 January 1999, with 325 distinct attributes (generally presence/absence) being captured. Ninety-nine companies had websites and 93 included pages dealing with some form of investor relations/financial information. 67% had a link from their home page directly to the investor relations page and 22 had a direct link to the latest annual report (p20).

The FASB (2000, pp21-23) study notes that 'one of the most significant decisions in designing financial and business reporting Web pages is the use of HTML and PDF file formats'[8]. (For a comprehensive comparison, see FASB (2000, p22)).

The study found that 21% of companies included their financial statements exclusively as PDF files, 58% used HTML, while 27% gave users full choice, providing the most flexibility. In addition to these popular formats, 12% also provided financial reports in word processor formats and 16% provided downloadable spreadsheet files of the financial statements (p23).

A second focus of the FASB study is on navigation aids. It noted that it is very easy to get 'lost in hyperspace' after clicking on several hyperlinks. Other navigation aids serve to reduce this problem. It was found that 71% of companies included a table of contents composed of hyperlinks so the user could go directly to a desired section; and 42% included 'next' and 'previous' buttons at the bottom of each page, so that the viewer could move through the annual report in a linear manner akin to the paper-based report (pp23-24).

Canada

A project undertaken for the Canadian Institute of Chartered Accountants (CICA) by Trites (1999a,b) surveyed the websites of 370 listed US and Canadian companies and considered the impact of technology on financial and business reporting. Among the issues considered are the difficulty in locating the boundary of the financial information, the need for easy export of information into user-designed models, and interactive reporting involving dialogue.

UK

In its survey of the websites of the FTSE 100 companies conducted in November 2000, *Financial Director* (2000) found that, in addition to HTML, 94 offer PDF[9], 24 offer Microsoft Powerpoint (especially useful for downloadable analyst presentations), 17 offer Excel spreadsheets, and 14 offer Word. It concluded that, *inter alia*, sites should have: a clear link from the homepage to corporate (and financial) information; should offer an email service; offer as many different formats as possible (including an HTML version so that the document can be skim read on the web and PDF to allow downloading); and hyperlinking of the notes to the accounts to the relevant sections of the accounts themselves.

International

Deller *et al.* (1999) surveyed the top 100 companies in each of the US, the UK and Germany. They reported that, in January 1998, the percentage having a website was 95%, 85% and 76%, respectively. In considering the scope of accounting information disclosed, they identified six categories: balance sheet data; profit and loss data; notes; cash flow data; interim reports; and financial time series data. The percentages providing balance sheet data are, respectively, 95%, 74% and 65%, while the corresponding percentages for profit and loss data are almost identical: 95%, 75%, and 63%. Greatest variation between countries occurs in relation to the provision of time series data, supplied by 95% of US companies but only 28% of UK companies and 21% of German companies.

When they looked at features of the sites, they found that very few sites have hyperlinked accounting data (7%, 38% and 13%, respectively) or financial data in processable format (13%, 6% and 7%, respectively). Rather more supply PDF (35%, 35% and 17%).

Taylor (1998) reported on a wide-ranging survey of 100 websites of some of the world's largest international companies. 83% included the company's annual report, with nearly half of these requiring the user to open the document in PDF format (requiring special software) and slightly more offering HTML text. Only 13% made their presentations to analysts (slides or text) available on-line. Taylor observed that ease of site navigation is critical, with the first level of site navigation beginning on the home page.

In a large-scale study by the IASC (1999), the Internet presence of 660 companies, comprising the 30 largest listed companies from 22 countries, was examined. It was found that 84% had websites and 62% had some form of financial disclosure. Based on their findings and a review of technological opportunities, the study made recommendations for electronic business reporting in both the short term and the longer term.

PricewaterhouseCoopers (2000) undertook a survey of the web-reporting practices of 60 best practice websites worldwide during July 2000. In terms of ease of access, they found that the investor relations section was one click away from the home page for 88% of sites and two clicks for the remaining 12%. 62% offered a site map and 72% search facilities. Two-way communications was offered by most companies, with 83% giving email addresses and 57% using broadcast emails (*ie* email alerts) to warn of new information. Investor/analyst presentations were available as follows: 63% offered slides; 37% offered audio versions; 25% offered visual versions; and 50% included an archive of these presentations. In terms of document formats offered in addition to HTML, 92% offered PDF, and only 8% offered a version that could be manipulated, such as Excel. Given that this is the most recent survey available at the time of writing, and that the companies surveyed were best practice web reporters, these findings represent the leading edge of current practice.

Stages in company reporting practices

Both the IASC (1999) and FASB (2000) studies identify three distinct types of company practice regarding the electronic distribution of business information. IASC describe three 'stages' of reporting: stage I where the printed financial statements are simply 'duplicated' in 'electronic paper' (*e.g.* PDF-Adobe Acrobat); stage II where HTML formatting is used, allowing hyperlinking and indexing; and stage III where electronic enhancements are used to present complex information in alternative ways (pp47-49). FASB identifies three 'philosophies' underpinning practice:

- it is seen as a *substitute* for printed material;
- it is seen as a *complement* to printed material; or
- it is seen as a way of innovating the business reporting package, in terms of new information contents and new tools (pp39-40).

These stages and philosophies appear to map on to each other.

The policy maker's dilemma

Cyert and Ijiri (1974) provided a useful analysis of the conflicts of interest that exist between various groups and the difficulty that these pose in the formulation of objectives for accounting. They examined three groups: the accounting profession; companies; and users. An information set is related to the interests of each, one set represents information that is useful to users, another represents information that companies are willing to disclose while a third represents information that auditors are capable of verifying. The three information sets can be thought of as intersecting circles - they do not fully overlap because of conflicts of interest (see Figure 2.1). These conflicts of interest arise because each group forms a different assessment of the cost-benefit trade off associated with information disclosure.

Figure 2.1 Key parties in the reporting process and conflicts of interest

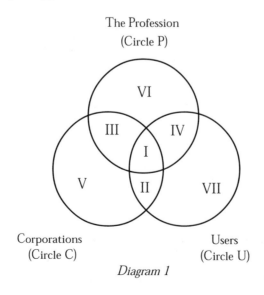

Diagram 1

Reprinted with permission. Cyert, R M and Ijiri Y, (1974), 'Problems of implementing the Trueblood objectives report', *Journal of Accounting Research*, Supplement diagram 1, p30. (© Institute of Professional Accounting, 1975)

The objective for policy makers is twofold. First, they must seek to provide an environment where the area of overlap (area I in Figure 2.1) is maximised, *i.e.* maximise the information set that users find useful, companies are willing to disclose and auditors can verify. Developments in information technology are helping here, as it becomes cheaper to capture and disseminate large amounts of information and sophisticated software agents allow users to analyse this without suffering from information overload. Policy makers can also assist by, for example, putting in place safe harbour legislation to encourage greater disclosure by companies and reform the liability laws for auditors so that they become more willing to offer an opinion on a greater range of information types.

Second, policy makers must act as arbiters in resolving the remaining conflicts of interest. They must decide whether to take a user-oriented approach, a company-oriented approach or an auditor-oriented approach. In recent years, the user-oriented approach has been most in evidence, reflecting shifting social attitudes to corporate responsibilities. This is not to say that policy makers always opt for the users' preferred solution, but rather that they have a predisposition to that group. For each issue, policy makers will weigh up the costs and benefits (direct and indirect) of different options for each group and then decide. Costs and benefits are weighted to favour the user group.

In the present study, the existence of conflicts of interest can be measured via statistical analysis of the questionnaire responses, specifically by assessing the level of across-group consensus. The questionnaire responses also allow the homogeneity of each group's views to be assessed (within-group consensus). This concept is not part of the Cyert and Ijiri framework.

Summary of key points

This chapter has summarised recent professional and academic debate and empirical evidence relevant to the discussion of web-based corporate reporting. The nineteenth century view of companies being accountable purely to their shareholders has given way to an acceptance that there are wider corporate accountabilities and, consequently, wider reporting obligations. Technological developments, especially the Internet, facilitate the discharge of these obligations by making it easy to disseminate a large amount of information structured in a variety of ways. Changes in business practices also argue for the dissemination of more information, presented in a way that can be interrogated based upon users' choices. Once again, technology acts in a facilitating capacity.

Surveys of company practice show that most companies are still at the first stage of web-based reporting, in other words they view the web report as a substitute for the printed report and merely duplicate the printed report on the web. No attempt is made to harness the power of the web to present complex information in alternative ways or offer new information content or information search and analysis tools. Projects and initiatives such as *Fauxcom* and XBRL point the way forward.

Finally, the underlying nature of the policy maker's dilemma was discussed. Because key interested parties have different perspectives, they often assess the costs and benefits of proposed changes to business reporting differently, generating conflicts of interest. The role of the regulator is to seek to minimise these conflicts and arbitrate on those that remain.

Endnotes:

[7] (http://www.ep.cs.nott.ac.uk/pdfcorner/noddypdf.html).

[8] The introduction to the *FauxCom* website and IASC (1999, pp26-30; 41-43; 48; and 74-75) make many of the same points.

[9] By contrast, Craven and Marston (1999, p327) report that in July 1998 (just over two years earlier) only 9 of the top 200 UK companies offered PDF.

CHAPTER THREE

COMPANY REPORTING OBLIGATIONS

This chapter begins by looking at the views of all 538 respondents (*i.e.* the combined groups) regarding the extent of a listed company's obligation to report to six key stakeholder groups. These groups are: customers; employees; suppliers; existing investors; potential investors; and the community/the public. It then considers, for each stakeholder group, the variation in views between the four main respondent groups. Finally, the extent to which each respondent group considers that private shareholders should be consulted on issues related to company external reporting is addressed.

Views of combined respondent groups

The column graph in Figure 3.1 shows the overall mean response to the question about the extent of listed companies' reporting obligations, displayed in descending order of importance. Not surprisingly, the obligation to existing investors comes first; this obligation is viewed as little short of 'absolute'. Then comes the obligation to potential investors and employees, which are ranked similarly between 'moderate' and 'major'. The final cluster of three stakeholder groups includes the community, suppliers and customers, which are all ranked between slight and moderate.

The dispersion of responses is shown in Table 3.1. As explained in chapter one, the standard deviation (SD) is used as the basis for describing the level of dispersion as follows: SD≤0.9 (very low); 0.9<SD≤1.0 (low); 1.0<SD≤1.1 (moderate); 1.1<SD≤1.2 (high); SD>1.2 (very high). It can be seen that there is most consensus regarding the obligation to existing investors and least consensus regarding that to potential investors.

Figure 3.1 Views of listed company reporting obligations

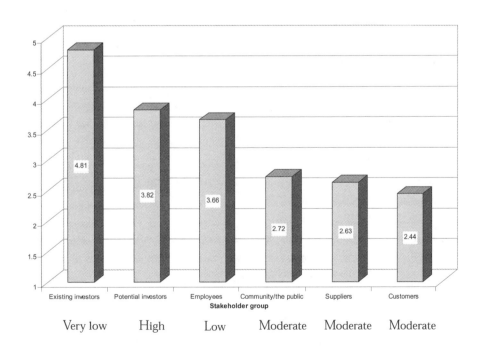

Variation in views between respondent groups

In this section, the views regarding each stakeholder group are considered in turn. Table 3.1 reports the mean and standard deviation for each respondent group in relation to each stakeholder group.

Table 3.1 Individual respondent group views regarding stakeholder groups - mean and standard deviation

Stakeholder group	Mean responses (dispersion)			
	Expert User	Private Shareholder	Finance Director	Audit Partner
Existing investors	4.84 Very low	4.75 Very low	4.88 Very low	4.82 Very low
Potential investors	3.92 High	3.69 High	4.06 Low	3.75 Moderate
Employees	3.84 Low	3.64 Moderate	3.58 Very low	3.33 Low
Community/the public	2.83 Moderate	2.60 High	2.91 Low	2.59 Very low
Suppliers	2.66 Moderate	2.57 Moderate	2.61 Very low	2.75 Very low
Customers	2.48 Moderate	2.36 High	2.53 Low	2.51 Low

Existing investors

The first row of Table 3.1 gives the summary results for each respondent group in relation to existing investors. A formal statistical test was conducted to see whether there existed a significant difference between the responses of the four main groups (see chapter 1, note 7 for details). The differences for this stakeholder group were not significant. Moreover, all four groups exhibited very low dispersion in their views.

The rationale for prioritising the reporting obligations to existing investors was explained by one audit partner in the following terms:

They are ultimately the owners of the company and I think that is who the ultimate obligation of the company is to ... clearly we can't go back to the nineteenth century and say no one else has any rights at all because particularly large listed companies are an important part of the overall economy, but there is, in my view, a fundamental difference between the ownership relationship and other relationships of varying strength. (audit partner)

Another audit partner, who separated out existing and potential investors together at the top, emphasised the availability of non-company sources of information:

These days there is so much information that people can access about companies, especially now that the Internet is in place. I think that people like suppliers and customers should make their own inquiries as suits their own situation as it's difficult to get a company to produce a report that meets all their individual needs. (audit partner)

This point was also made by a fund manager:

We didn't really see any need to provide information for customers or suppliers. It was up to them to ferret for what information they could. (expert user)

Yet another audit partner considered that wider disclosures were commercially unacceptable:

People who are running larger organisations now have to be aware that there is this broader church of people who have legitimate interests but there's a line to be drawn and I guess it's a line of commerciality...how much information do you share with the customer about a specific product or its performance or whatever? (audit partner)

Potential investors

Table 3.1, row 2 shows the summary results in relation to potential investors. The differences observed between the views of the four respondent groups were significant at the 5% level. The level of dispersion of views varied considerably within groups, ranging from the finance director group, which exhibited low dispersion, to both user groups which exhibited high dispersion.

Employees

Table 3.1, row 3 shows the summary results for employees. The differences observed between the views of the four respondent groups were significant at the 1% level. The dispersion of views did not exceed 'moderate' for any group.

One finance director who rated the obligation to employees as absolute referred to the German model of corporate governance:

The dominance of the German lobby in Euro legislation is almost bound to result in the gradual creeping of the socialisation of corporate governance ... employee representation and all the rest of it. (finance director)

Two investment analysts who rated employees equally to investors justified this in relation to the importance of intellectual capital to many businesses:

Unless you carry your employees with you then the success of the business can be compromised, now that intellectual capital is actually the core element in a lot of companies. (expert user)

Employees are much more significant than you might have immediately assumed, given things like intellectual capital. (expert user)

Community/the public

Table 3.1, row 4 provides the summary results for each respondent group in relation to the community/the public. The differences observed between the views of the four respondent groups were significant at the 5% level. Dispersion of views varied considerably within groups, ranging from audit partners having very low dispersion to private shareholders having high dispersion.

One finance director who rated the obligation to this group as 'major' explained:

[X] *is a big local employer and the impact of some of its projects on people who have to live around construction sites while they are in operation means that* [X] *really does take into account its responsibilities to the local community* (finance director)

Suppliers

Table 3.1, row 5 provides the summary results for each respondent group in relation to suppliers. The differences observed between the views of the four respondent groups were not significantly different. The dispersion of views did not exceed 'moderate' for any group.

One audit partner who, unusually, ranked suppliers equal with investors and employees, explained as follows:

When you look at some of the major companies these days, they are less and less an isolated entity that only has shareholders to deal with ... there are a lot of strategic alliances where the other organisation's success is linked to the success of your own ... so I think the whole supply chain, end to end, is becoming increasingly important in understanding the relationships. (audit partner)

Customers

Finally, Table 3.1, row 6 gives the summary results regarding customers. The differences for this stakeholder group were not significantly different. The dispersion of views within groups varied considerably.

A corporate lender who ranked customers below investors, employees and suppliers explained:

It's the old stakeholder argument. Although an investor makes a financial investment in a company, an employee makes a physical investment ... and suppliers also have a stake in the company. ...Customers just take the service and disappear – what differentiates them is length of relationship. (expert user)

General observation

It is noticeable, and perhaps not surprising, that the dispersion of responses within the finance director and audit partner groups is never higher than that for the two user groups. Thus, as distinct groups, finance directors and audit partners generally agree on the extent of companies' reporting obligations to the different stakeholder groups, whereas users' views, especially those of private shareholders, vary more.

Need to consult private shareholders

Respondents were asked the extent to which they agreed that private shareholders should be consulted on issues to do with company external reporting. The response scale was from 1 (strongly agree) to 5 (strongly disagree), with 3 representing a neutral view. The distribution of results is shown in Figure 3.2 in a 100% divided bar graph. The group mean and dispersion is shown to the right hand side of the graph.

Figure 3.2 Need to consult private shareholders

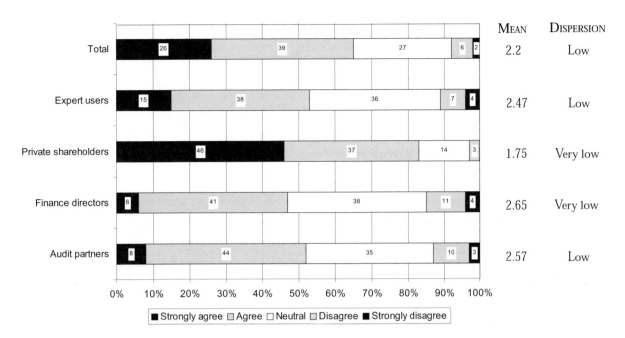

On average, the four groups agree that private shareholders should be consulted, despite their possible lack of knowledge regarding business reporting issues (*i.e.* the means are less than 3). Not surprisingly, the group at the centre of the question, private shareholders, agree most strongly, with 83% expressing a positive view. The other group's views are closer to a neutral position. These differences between the groups' responses are found to be highly significant (at the 0.1% level).

Those who disagreed with consultation expressed the following reasons:

There is a practicality issue about consulting with private shareholders, but equally as a private shareholder myself I actually get a little bit fed up with a number of the consultation initiatives that are sent to me by companies I'm involved with as a private shareholder. Frankly I feel that there are esteemed bodies that are quite capable of shaping the agenda for me as a private investor. (audit partner)

The private shareholder increasingly understands less of the bigger issues that are facing the company...in terms of corporate governance my experience is that they are not up to the task. (expert user)

A more neutral position was justified thus:

I suppose I'm protecting the companies' interests here in terms of competitive advantage...I get concerned that sometimes what the private shareholder would want is not necessarily in the best interests of the company...you can buy and sell your shares tomorrow and you've therefore got no allegiance to the company. (audit partner)

Those who agreed referred to the avoidance of bad publicity, the danger of antagonising this group, and fairness:

We are quite happy to have these kind of consultations and in fact we'd rather do that and pick up issues before they arise than be hit with them after. (finance director)

In the 80s, [X] *responded to analyst demands for more and more information so that its report got bigger and bigger ... then it found that what satisfied the analyst community was really getting up the noses of a lot of their ordinary public shareholders because the report and accounts was getting ridiculous.* (expert user)

It is essential in the interests of fairness ... I don't see why companies as well as regulators shouldn't have a role in this consultation process. (expert user)

People who aren't grouped together in big bodies with some sort of clout get ignored. (private shareholder)

Private shareholders are disadvantaged versus institutions in the UK. (private shareholder)

Summary of key points

The questionnaire results presented in this chapter reveal a very high level of consensus both within and across respondent groups regarding the reporting obligations that a listed company has in relation to various stakeholder groups. All respondent groups give priority to existing investors, with 84% rating the obligation as 'absolute'. Potential investors and employees are next most important: 73% of respondents rate the obligation to potential investors as 'major' or 'absolute', while the figure for employees is 63%. The community/public, suppliers and customers come next, the percentage of respondents rating the obligation as 'major' or 'absolute' are 20%, 18% and 14%, respectively.

During interviews, the reasons given for this pattern relate to the investors as ultimate owners, the increasingly important role of employees (in terms of corporate governance and intellectual capital), the availability of other information sources for non-investor groups, and the potential commercial disadvantage in disclosing information relevant to non-investor groups.

By contrast, there was considerable variation across the respondent groups regarding the extent to which private shareholders should be consulted on issues related to company external reporting. Private shareholders strongly agreed whereas the other groups' level of agreement was generally mild. The interviews elicited a range of points, both in support and against. These included arguments about fairness and the avoidance of bad publicity, loss of competitive advantage due to excessive demands for the disclosure of information, and lack of interest and understanding on the part of private shareholders.

CHAPTER FOUR

ATTITUDES TO ICAS (1999) PROPOSALS RE WEB-BASED REPORTING

The ICAS (1999) discussion document offered explicit proposals regarding the content, structure and frequency of web-based business reporting packages. This chapter presents and discusses the views of users, preparers and auditors regarding these proposals. It should be noted that some of these proposals subsume those made by others, such as Elliott (1992; 1994) and Wallman (1995; 1997). A final section investigates the relationship between respondents' familiarity with the Internet and their stated attitudes and preferences.

General amount and type of information

ICAS (1999) proposed, broadly consistent with the recommendations in *Making Corporate Reports Valuable* (ICAS, 1988), that an electronic library-type resource, based on the corporate database used by management, be made available to external users. This proposal addresses the general amount and type of information that is made publicly available. Figure 4.1 reproduces the specific question asked and graphs the distribution of respondents' views; the mean and dispersion are shown in a panel on the right hand side of the graph.

Figure 4.1 Requirement to disclose key information

Question: *To what extent do you agree that a company should be required to make available key information that it uses to manage the company (subject to legitimate concerns re commercial confidentiality and risk of misinterpretation).*

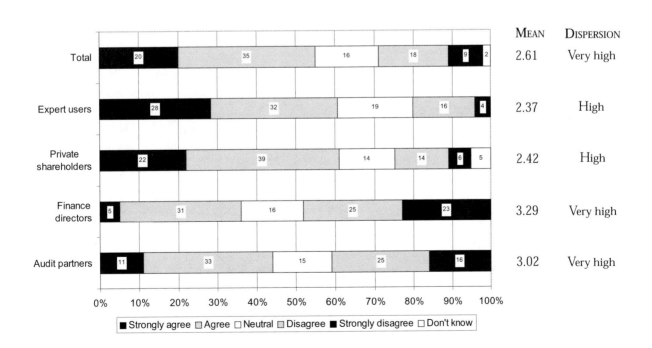

Not surprisingly, both user groups, on average, are reasonably strongly in agreement that management should make key management information available (subject to legitimate concerns), while finance directors are mildly against this and audit partners are neutral. The differences between the groups' views are significant at the 0.1% level. However, despite their average disagreement, 36% of finance directors respond positively to this proposal, so there appears to be little consensus among the group (dispersion is indeed very high).

Those who agreed with this proposal focused on the usefulness of the information and ease with which more information can now be provided, as well as referring to the need for regulation to ensure consistency of information provision. For example:

There is potentially a great deal of information that would be useful. (expert user)

We don't have much about the way in which we authorise our capital expenditure and control our cash and so on ... there are a number of things that could be done that would enhance people's understanding without concerning commercial confidentiality. (audit partner)

Once you've got the website set up then it's easier to extend the use of it. (expert user)

If there is a requirement to disclose the following information then you can compare apples with apples... I do think that having standardised information is helpful. (audit partner)

Those who disagreed seemed most concerned about commercial confidentiality problems, despite the attempt to exclude this issue from the question. For example:

Commercial confidentiality is a major problem. (audit partner)

In a previous job in the textile sector we were operating with particularly large single customer contracts and on incredibly fine margins. If our competitors knew exactly what our margins were, they would be very interested to know exactly what our supply routes were and how we were getting those margins. We were operating in a global marketplace where other players operate under their disclosure requirements which can be a lot less progressive. (finance director)

Structure of database

ICAS (1999) proposed that existing technology be exploited to layer and link information, while maintaining a facility for free search. The two questions covered in this section address these issues of how information is structured and accessed by users. The question addressed in Figure 4.2 asks about layering.

Figure 4.2 Requirement to layer information

Question: To what extent do you agree that companies should be required to layer information to avoid information overload, while providing the detail desired by many (i.e. overview in top layer, becoming progressively more complex and detailed in lower layers).

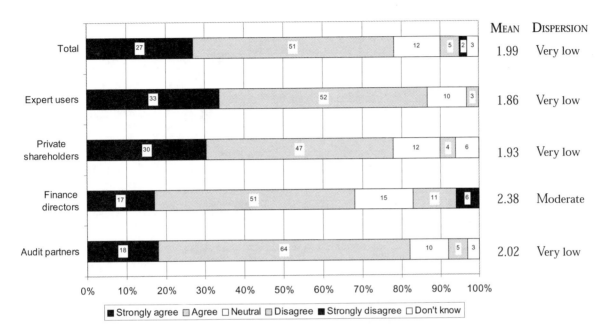

All groups agree, with reasonably high within-group consensus, that it is desirable to layer information to avoid information overload. Interestingly, expert users and private shareholder views are closely aligned and strongly in agreement with this requirement. It may be that the aspect of layering valued by expert users, who are less likely to suffer from information overload, is the structure imposed, while private shareholders value more the ability to restrict their view of the data to a broad overview.

Finance directors, though least strongly in agreement with this proposal, still offer reasonably strong support, as do audit partners. While 68% of finance directors are positive, 17% are negative, resulting in moderate dispersion of views. The differences between the groups' views are significant at the 0.1% level.

Respondents supported this proposal because of the ability of layering to enhance communicative effectiveness, to mitigate information overload and the increasing complexity of reporting, and to serve multiple audiences (all of which are linked). For example:

> [Layering] *appeals to me in terms of getting across the information…it is very important for the private client. The danger is that it passes an editorial control over to the companies which I'm not totally happy with.* (expert user)

> *I've just thrown half a dozen weighty annual reports out because there were better things to do, plus for ignoramuses like me a lot of it is over my head.* (private shareholder)

> *You can start with some overall information about the company as a whole and then start drilling down … Part of the problem with reporting at the moment is the increasing complexity makes it very difficult for users to really get an understanding as to what's going on.* (audit partner)

> *I'm very much in favour of the layering of information as a means of making the information available to those who want it, without overloading those who don't.* (expert user)

The question in Figure 4.3 asks about free search.

Figure 4.3 Requirement to maintain free search facility

Question: *To what extent do you agree that companies should be required to maintain a facility on their website for free search (e.g. via provision of a search box), allowing users to retain control over the search and selection process (i.e. search software should support user-defined queries).*

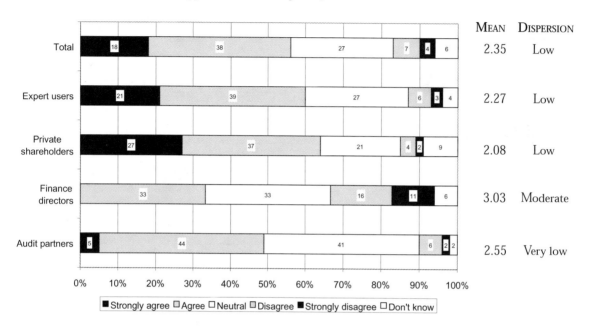

Once again, users were, on average, most strongly in favour of this requirement, exhibiting reasonably strong support. Finance directors were, as a group, neutral, though they exhibited the highest degree of dispersion (moderate), with 33% responding positively and 27% responding negatively. It would appear that some finance directors prefer to 'guide' the user through the information, perhaps fearing that an unstructured interrogation of the database by the user will result in an incomplete or biased view. Audit partners' views lay, on average, between those of users and finance directors. The differences between the groups' views are significant at the 0.1% level.

Use of templates to provide pre-packaged information

A specific ICAS (1999) proposal was that a range of pre-packaged information be provided, based on a standardised template for each stakeholder group. This template would contain core information of relevance to all stakeholders plus a set of additional information of particular relevance to the interests and needs of the individual stakeholder group. This idea is very similar to Elliott's (1994) concept of 'views'. Figure 4.4 shows respondents' views.

Figure 4.4 Requirement to provide pre-packaged information

Question: *To what extent do you agree that companies should be required to provide a range of pre-packaged information, based on a standardised template for each group of users, specified by an external regulatory body.*

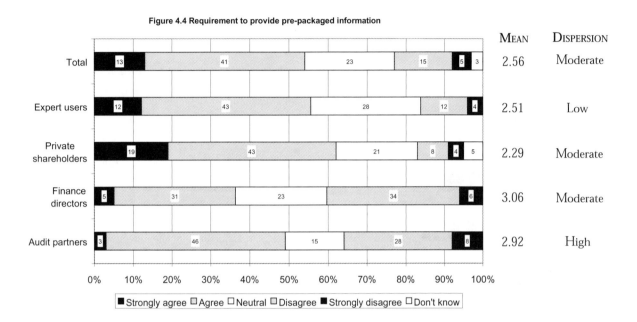

Figure 4.4 Requirement to provide pre-packaged information

Although, on average, both user groups (especially private shareholders) favour this idea, support is only 'mild' for expert users. Finance directors and audit partners are, on average, neutral. It is to be expected that private shareholders, as non professionals, would benefit most from this proposal. The differences between the groups' views are significant at the 0.1% level.

Concerns regarding pre-packaging related to issues of cost, information equality across groups and the perceived disadvantages of over regulation:

It's cost again. It would be more work for the company. I think the user has to take some responsibility for selecting what they want. (expert user)

It's important that it is the same set of information that's available to everyone. (expert user)

I'm quite happy to see the mandatory inclusion of certain items of content but I think management should be left to its own devices as to how it presents that and the bias that it wishes to give. (expert user)

Reducing unfair advantage and widening access

The next ICAS (1999) proposal involving the Internet concerned extending access to company meetings and to management. Four specific questions were asked - three concerning general meetings and one concerning one-to-one meetings. The results regarding general meetings are shown in Figures 4.5 to 4.7.

Figure 4.5 Requirement to place records of general meetings on web

Question: *To what extent do you agree that companies should, to reduce unfair advantage, be required to extend access to <u>general</u> company meetings with financial analysts/institutional shareholders by placing records (i.e. presentation packs and slides) on website.*

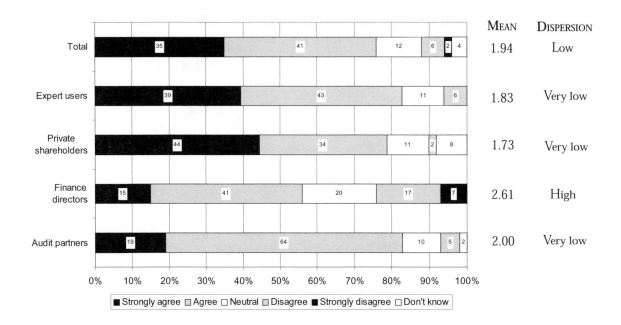

Figure 4.6 Requirement to place audio-visual record of general meetings on web

Question: *To what extent do you agree that companies should, to reduce unfair advantage, be required to extend access to <u>general</u> company meetings with financial analysts/institutional shareholders by archiving an audio-visual record on website.*

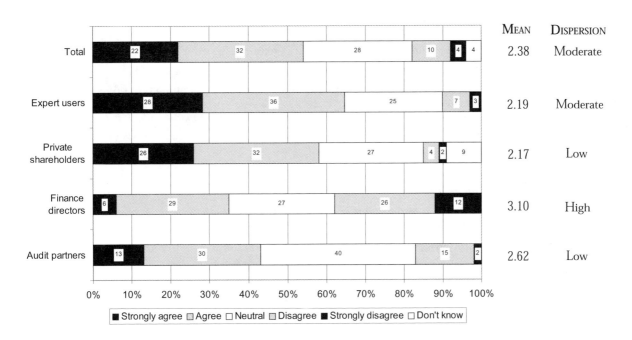

Figure 4.7 Requirement to broadcast general meetings

Question: *To what extent do you agree that companies should, to reduce unfair advantage, be required to extend access to <u>general</u> company meetings with financial analysts' institutional shareholders by broadcasting live via satellite television channel or video webcast.*

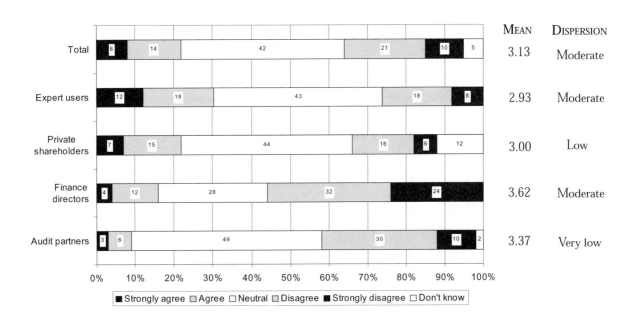

General meetings

In relation to general meetings, on average all groups strongly agree (with the exception of finance directors whose level of agreement is mild) that the records of general meetings be placed on the website. This is something that some companies are already doing. Both user groups, on average, reasonably strongly favour archiving an audio-visual record of these meetings. Audit partners offer mild support while finance directors are neutral.

Perhaps surprisingly, however, there is no general support from *any* group for webcasting (or broadcasting *via* satellite television) these meetings – both user groups are, on average, neutral whilst finance directors and audit partners are against (audit partners mildly and finance directors reasonably strongly). It is interesting to note, therefore, that these emerging practices are noted, with favour, by FASB (2000, p*ix* and p12).

The many who support the extension of access to general meetings comment along the following lines:

There is a lot of discussion that happens between institutions and boards of companies which is not generally available and I think with better communications such as the web there is no excuse for not making information available to everybody almost instantaneously. (finance director)

We already do it … we publish our full accounts and interims on the web on the day we announce at 7.30 in the morning as well as the analysts' presentation pack. (finance director)

I suspect we probably wouldn't use it very often but there may be occasions where we would like to see what was there … this really ought to be available to everybody. (expert user– fund manager)

The communications revolution has actually eroded those advantages that professional investors have over members of the general public, but I don't think this is actually a negative thing. You make money by better processing of information. (expert user–investment analyst)

The game is changing at such a pace of knots that there is less excuse for not making information available. (expert user)

One finance director who generally supported extending access was, however, concerned that the audio-visual record could change the nature of the meeting for the worse:

It's whether or not it changes the tone of the actual meeting. If the boss says something silly then it's easy to call all the fellows afterwards and say 'Here, wait a minute, [name] didn't mean it that way he meant it this way.' I suppose it's feeling uncomfortable about control moving away from us and therefore having to be far more structured in what we do. (finance director)

Another respondent expressed a similar concern:

I think that, regardless of the class of investor, they should have free access to the information. There is a problem – there are some 'enthusiastic' private investors that can destroy a normal communication path between a company and professional investors. We are starting to see that in some of the Internet conference calls: if they were opened up to a wider group then you could destroy their value. (expert user)

Another view expressed was that equal access was an unattainable goal:

It does seem a bit unrealistic to expect that information about every publicly quoted company can be distributed equally to every individual who has an interest … It seems inevitable, whatever regulations they put in, nods and winks will occur. (private shareholder)

It is interesting to note that a recent study by Arthur Andersen (2001) found that, among the top 25 FTSE companies, 21 (84%) were placing placing audio or video webcasts or slides from analysts' presentations (mainly those given at the annual or bi-annual results presentations) on their websites.

One-to-one meetings

In relation to one-to-one meetings, it is apparent that there is an extreme difference between the views of the four groups (see Figure 4.8).

Figure 4.8 Requirement to place minutes of one-to-one meetings on web

Question To what extent do you agree that companies should be required to extend access to <u>one-to-one</u> meetings by placing detailed minutes on website, to reduce unfair advantage.

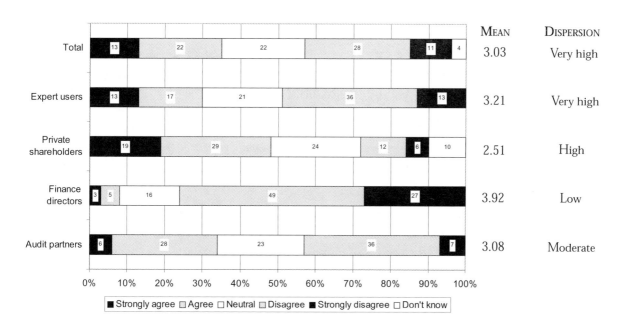

The two user groups are, unusually, very divided in their views. On average, expert users are mildly against the proposal to place detailed minutes on the website while private shareholders are mildly in favour, although the dispersion in views is at least 'high' in both cases. This result is perhaps not surprising, as one-to-one meetings are the source of potential comparative information advantage for expert users, especially information intermediaries such as sell-side investment analysts. What is perhaps surprising is that 30% of expert users do in fact *support* this proposal. Although audit partners are, on average, neutral, finance directors are strongly opposed (only 8% are positive, with 76% negative). In fact, this represents the strongest opposition to any of the ICAS proposals to come from any group.

Those who agreed with the proposal were swayed principally by the apparent unfairness of the current situation:

The analyst has the advantage in terms of information and they are not using that to protect the shareholders in general, so I think if information's going to come into the market place, it should be available to all shareholders simultaneously. (audit partner)

There's one finance director of a public company that we act for and he is very candid with me when we discuss the extent to which analysts and suchlike have the privilege to access company information and yet it doesn't seem to make the analysts much better at their jobs… The existence of the unfairness rankles with me. (audit partner)

29

If you're an investor you don't want to find out something after somebody's already dealt and that's what happens ... That's just wholly unacceptable. (expert user)

What will happen is a company will talk to its tame stockbroker and disclose information which is only disclosed by them to their mates and not put in the public domain. (private shareholder)

Others felt that public disclosure could be self defeating:

We would expect to have our own meetings with the company and I wouldn't expect to have those meetings put on record ... I need to have a full understanding about the company, and they probably wouldn't be willing to share quite so much information if they thought that the whole meeting was going to be on record ... It could be quite dangerous. (expert user– corporate lender)

I think it would alter the tenor of the meeting ... you quite often get asked about individuals and the strength of them and while you probably shouldn't be venturing these personal opinions, they are personal opinions and you can have these kinds of conversations. (finance director)

If you say place detailed minutes of one-to-one meetings, then the point of having them disappears. In many of these one-to-one meetings we use our influence, if you like, to steer a management in a particular direction ... it wouldn't be something that we would be comfortable with if it were then going to be made public. (expert user – fund manager)

Holland (1998a;b) provides a useful insight into finance directors and expert users' perceptions of such meetings. They are seen as facilitating a 'dual knowledge advantage', whereby the existence of external monitoring by financial institutions sharpens up the process of internal debate (1998a, p261). Companies expressed the view that, if such meetings became open (as they would if minutes were placed on the web), many of the relationship advantages would be lost (Holland, 1998b, p51). This view was expressed by one of our interviewees in the following manner:

It can be a two-way corridor – one of the reasons I moved across into management consultancy was that we were doing a lot of work that was of great interest to finance directors and corporate strategy people. It was another view of things – another source of insight and information for them. So it can be a two-way relationship. (expert user)

Annual general meetings (AGMs)

The future role of AGMs has been the subject of considerable debate in recent years, with many of the arguments being captured in the DTI Consultation Document *Company General Meetings and Shareholder Communication* (DTI, 1999) and the Company Law Review (DTI 2000a, pp92-104). Following consultation, the overall conclusion is that AGMs should not be abolished, but that developments in technology should be used to preserve their essential functions while avoiding acknowledged defects. Instead, it is suggested that technology be used to hold dispersed meetings, connected by communication links (DTI, 2000a, para. 4.31).

The ICAS proposal to webcast AGMs is consistent with this suggestion, although it does not allow two-way communication. In this context, it is interesting to note that a US survey has shown that, in mid 1999, 10% of the survey population currently used the Internet to broadcast annual meetings, with a further 25% actively considering it (reported in FASB, 2000, p8).

This survey asks two questions about AGMs (see Figures 4.9 and 4.10).

Figure 4.9 Requirement to webcast AGM

Question: To what extent do you agree that companies should teleconference (i.e. webcast) company AGMs to allow
wider access.

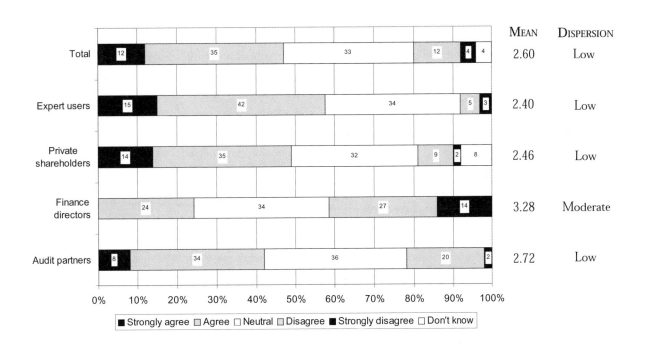

Figure 4.10 Requirement to replace AGM with online questioning

Question: To what extent do you agree that companies should be required to replace company AGMs by a facility for
online questioning on management by users and conduct voting online.

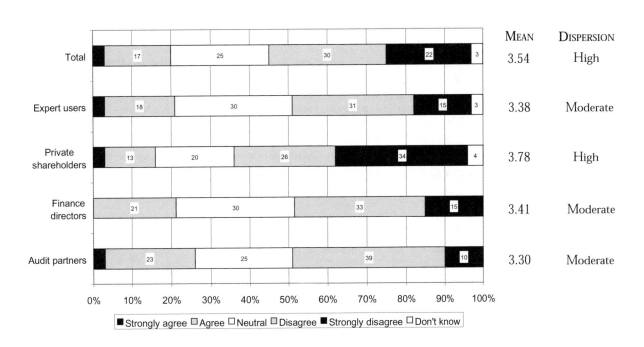

Both user groups, on average, supported the ICAS proposal to webcast the AGM, as did audit partners (though less strongly). Finance directors mildly opposed the proposal. Company management carefully rehearses company meetings, but AGMs can be unpredictable. Perhaps management feared the consequences of disseminating unwelcome questions more widely. The level of dispersion of views within groups was generally 'low' (the exception being the finance director group).

The more radical ICAS proposal to replace company AGMs by a facility for online questioning of management and online voting was, on average, rejected by all groups. With the exception of private shareholders, the level of rejection was 'mild'; however private shareholders expressed reasonably strong disagreement. For all four groups, however, the level of dispersion was 'moderate' or 'high'. This view is perhaps not surprising since AGMs cater, in the main, to small shareholders. There are perhaps three (not necessarily mutually exclusive) reasons why private shareholders wish to retain the AGM. They may perceive it as a valuable vehicle for eliciting useful information about the company; they may also see it as an effective component of corporate governance; they may also simply like the 'occasion' – the chance to have an outing with perhaps a free gift thrown in.

Interviewees who were against replacing the AGM with online questioning focused on their value as a control mechanism and a source of useful information, questioned the need to replace rather than supplement AGMs, or were unsettled by the de-humanising aspect of online questioning.

I think the boards of companies are faceless enough individuals as it is and I think it does them and the shareholders quite a good service to stand them up in front of a group of people for questioning. I don't think to replace the AGM is right, though I think you can add to it with online questioning. (finance director)

Businesses are still collections of people, not phantom entities that don't have any reality. So I don't see how you can avoid having some sort of general meeting at intervals of at least a couple of years. (private shareholder)

AGMs can be extremely ineffective, but I'm very wary of throwing away something that's a couple of hundred years old without being absolutely confident that you are going to replace it with something that is better. Anyway, in practical terms I think it would be almost impossible to achieve online questioning – I mean, when is management going to make itself available? (expert user)

I don't object to doing that in addition, but to scrap the AGM where you actually have the opportunity to personally talk to and meet the senior management would be a very bad thing in my view ... I actually go to a number of AGMs and I actually find it quite useful. The problem with non-spontaneous events is they end up being managed by the management. Only at a completely open forum can you actually get significant questions answered or spring them on the management when they are not expecting them. (private shareholder)

Those who favoured online questioning often based this view on their experiences of AGMs rendered ineffective either by their scripted format or by the quirky nature of questions:

I've attended a number of AGMs over my time and I have a fairly jaundiced view ... Any positive development away from the script formats that we have at the moment towards a more open and accessible format is going to be a better thing. (audit partner)

AGMs can be a nightmare where people, shareholders with very few shares, bring their particular problems to the meeting – some of them may have a political agenda. (expert user)

One finance director embraced very positively the two-way dialogue afforded by online questioning. His experience with online questioning and chatrooms is worth reproducing in full:

[finance director] *I actually think that there is a popularisation vehicle now growing in strength, very fast, through corporate websites, that is absolutely going to break this one open. Our Chief Exec/Chairman and myself are very keen on the idea of moving to something that is becoming increasingly common in the States, which is almost moving away from analyst briefings and getting into more of a chat room environment. What you actually do is, if you're putting a briefing presentation pack together, … you put it on your website and you make yourself available between the hours of X and X to respond to any queries that <u>any</u> shareholder may have on that information.*

[interviewer] *So your company's very positive about that. I can see it being time consuming, having to reply individually to people.*

[finance director] *But what do you think two days spent tramping round the City is? That is what I did on Monday and Tuesday of this week. We went to see the same eight people whom we go and see each interim and final, and that process is <u>just</u> as burdensome and time consuming. But the issue with that one is that it's the same eight faces. Yes, they happen to represent 80% of our share register and therefore the popularist in you, frankly, gets knocked into touch by the 80/20 rule. The big lions have got the biggest bark but at the end of the day, I think the momentum behind this thing is going to be very powerful, in that those companies that <u>haven't</u> got something like that will find that people will start getting the knives out to them. We are an unusual company because, amongst a certain community of investors, we are a very visible stock. And if you look on the US chatrooms, apparently we're one of the most discussed UK companies. Now, what we actually find is that through our investor relations website, which at the moment is just a very bog-standard one as we literally just post up all the stuff that gets onto the stock exchange, we get quite a lot of communication in. People want to know about the company and they are very happy to use the investor relations email to say "What's happening to the share price? Why did this happen?".*

[interviewer] *And you would typically respond to these things, would you?*

[finance director] *Yes. Well, it's an interesting balance between whether we just let it happen in chatrooms or whether we intervene, because there is no doubt that you can get yourself into a dangerous position if you feel you have to respond to every bit of chit-chat that is going on. What I actually find is that the users sort of regulate themselves. We have an investor relations site with the ability to email us on it, <u>and</u> there are various chat rooms where people can gossip to their hearts content. What we find is that the cross over between the two - that is to say people asking silly gossipy questions through the investor relations bit - doesn't really happen. The people who ask the questions through the investor relations bit normally ask fairly sensible balanced questions. They are either investors or would be investors. If they are sensible and balanced questions I am quite happy to respond or at least to guide my colleagues in which way I'd like them to respond.*

These management experiences of online questioning indicate that, for this company at least, there are no real practical constraints to the process.

Within this section, the differences between the groups' views to all six questions asked are significant at the 0.1% level. This indicates the very different views held by the four main groups with regard to these issues.

Frequency of updating of web data

The survey conducted in ICAS (1999) found that those involved in corporate reporting saw advantages to regular, periodic reporting. Market makers preferred the structure and discipline of periodic review linked to reporting cycles and were only moderately dissatisfied with the timeliness of business information flows. This is somewhat at odds with the common assertion that there is demand for continuous (or real-time) reporting. Figures 4.11 and 4.12 relate to this issue.

Question: *To what extent do you agree that companies should update business reporting information on websites periodically (e.g. quarterly or monthly), not continuously.*

Figure 4.11 Requirement to update website information periodically

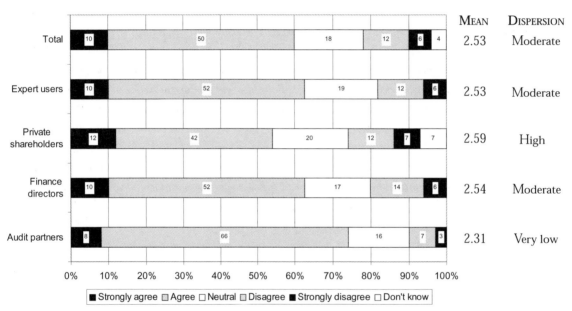

	MEAN	DISPERSION
Total	2.53	Moderate
Expert users	2.53	Moderate
Private shareholders	2.59	High
Finance directors	2.54	Moderate
Audit partners	2.31	Very low

■ Strongly agree □ Agree □ Neutral □ Disagree ■ Strongly disagree □ Don't know

Figure 4.12 Requirement to disclose frequency of updating

Question: To what extent do you agree that companies should be required to distinguish clearly information that is continuously updated from more stable information that is updated only periodically.

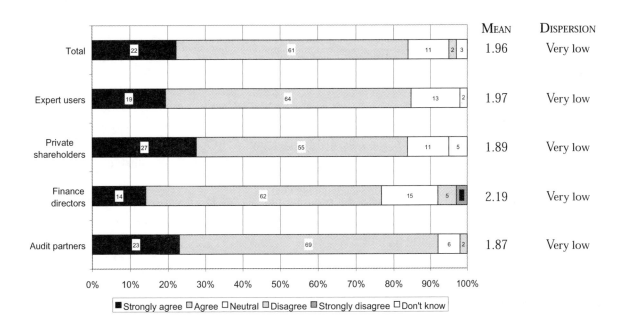

Responses seem to support the ICAS view, as all groups agree (either mildly or reasonably strongly) that more frequent, periodic updating is preferable, with no significant differences between the groups. It is interesting to note that audit partners, who most strongly support this proposal, display very low dispersion (two-thirds respond 'agree').

Those interviewees who agreed with the proposal to update only periodically cited the suitability of periodic reporting for efficient working practices:

If one structures things around sensible calendar intervals, everybody can work towards it, everybody knows where they are ... and that makes planning a lot easier. (expert user)

The problem with continuous reporting is that you don't know when new information will appear ... you don't want to have to go round a website everyday just to see if there's anything new there. If there is any news I'd much rather have it distributed by email. (private shareholder)

Richardson and Scholz (2000) identify two other possible reasons (one technological, the other legal) why continuous reporting is unlikely in the near future. The first is that companies' out-dated internal systems are unable to support continuous reporting – the introduction of enterprise-wide systems is a prerequisite. They offer the following anecdotal evidence to support this argument:

Consider the revenue reporting process of one anonymous Fortune 500 company. Disparate reporting systems are maintained by each of the company's ten divisions. Furthermore, these "systems" often consist of several unrelated programs within the division or enterprise (a sub-unit of a division). For example, one enterprise within one division uses three separate modules to determine their sales figure. The modules are a chaotic mix of legacy systems that are not based on similar platforms, languages or terms.

The enterprise's accounting department downloads the output of these three systems into a Microsoft Access database that is used to generate an enterprise-level sales report. To obtain division-level sales data, the Access reports must be combined with other enterprises' results in an Excel spreadsheet. This is done weekly. Determining corporate-wide sales figures requires yet another manual transfer of information from the divisions' various general ledger systems to a completely separate corporate consolidation reporting system. This is done only at the end of each month, and takes nearly a week to complete. Even then, the process is considered a "soft close", which means that the accounts have not been thoroughly reconciled or closely scrutinised. A "hard close" is performed at quarter end. It takes over a week to complete and usually results in significant changes to the "soft" numbers. (pp155-156)

The second constraint on continuous reporting is legal. In the Richardson and Scholz (2000) study, all investor relations directors interviewed 'stated that their policy is to post only data that have already been vetted through established procedures to minimise the potential for creating additional litigation risk' (p156). It has, of course, to be recognised that these comments come from people working in the US, which is acknowledged to be a much more litigious society than the UK.

Interviewees in this study who disagreed with the proposal for increased, but periodic, reporting cited the consequences of providing more frequent reports and the extra workload that more frequent periodic reporting and continuous reporting would seem to require:

In our business the analysts can virtually tell what your profit is going to be once they know how your house sales have been. If we start providing them with quarterly information on house sales, we would actually have to tell them a heck of a lot more about the business to avoid them going away and drawing the wrong conclusions ... I think the whole workload question has also got to come into it ... the FTSE 100 companies have the technical expertise and the resources to be able to comply with some of these best practice things. (finance director)

What you have to recognise is the amount of effort that actually goes into reporting and getting that reporting right. (audit partner)

A supplementary question, suggested by Xiao *et al.* (2000, p12), queried the importance of distinguishing clearly information that is continuously updated from more stable information that is updated only periodically. (see Figure 4.12). There was strong support from three of the groups to this proposal (finance directors' support was reasonably strong). Moreover, there was also very low dispersion within each group. Clearly there is substantial consensus that this is an important principle. The differences between the groups' views are significant at the 1% level.

Impact of familiarity with the Internet

Table 4.1 shows how familiar respondents were with the Internet. Across all responses, 60% used the Internet almost daily; however the frequency of use varied markedly between the four primary groups. The most frequent users were expert users (84% used almost daily), while the least frequent users were private shareholders (41% used almost daily). Finance directors and audit partners fell in between these two groups. Statistically, private shareholders were significantly less frequent Internet users than each of the other three groups.

Table 4.1 Internet use by respondents

Group	Percentage of respondents			
	Never	**Rarely**	**About once weekly**	**Almost daily**
Expert user	-	3	13	84
Private shareholder	27	12	20	41
Finance director	1	11	22	66
Audit partner	3	7	31	59
Total	**12**	**9**	**19**	**60**

Perhaps surprisingly, however, the correlations between frequency of Internet use and responses to the ICAS proposals were not generally very high[10]. More frequent Internet users were associated (at the 5% level, at least,) with stronger agreement with the following six questions: requirement to disclose key information; requirement to layer information; requirements (three) re general meetings; and requirement to replace AGM with online questioning. The highest correlation was with the requirement to replace AGM with online questioning – a correlation of -0.23. This response is perhaps driven by the attitudes of those less familiar with the Internet, who would lose *de facto* access to the shareholder democratic process under this proposal.

Overview and summary of key points

To form a basis for summarising the key points to emerge from the findings presented in this chapter, three tables have been prepared that provide an overview of respondents' reactions to the ICAS (1999) proposals. Table 4.2 presents, in descending order of agreement, the combined mean response to the twelve proposals. All but three proposals receive, on average, at least mild support from the combined group.

Table 4.2 Combined mean response to the ICAS (1999) proposals

Proposal	Mean response[1]	Descriptive label
Place records of general meetings on web	1.94	Strong agreement
Disclose frequency of updating	1.96	
Layer information	1.99	
Maintain free search facility	2.35	Reasonably strong agreement
Place audio-visual record of general meetings on web	2.38	
Update website periodically, not continuously	2.53	Mild agreement
Provide pre-packaged information	2.56	
Webcast AGM	2.60	
Disclose key information	2.61	
Place minutes of one-to-one meetings on web	3.03	Neutral
Broadcast general meetings	3.13	
Replace AGM with online questioning	3.54	Mild disagreement

Note 1: Mean responses are shown in descending order of agreement.

Table 4.3 focuses on the level of within-group and across-group consensus. Somewhat crudely, 'very low', 'low' and 'moderate' dispersion has been taken to indicate the presence of consensus within a group, while 'high' and 'very high' dispersion has been taken to indicate the absence of consensus. Where the differences between the four groups are statistically significant at the 5% level, this has been taken to indicate a lack of consensus across groups.

Table 4.3 Patterns of within-group and across-group consensus observed

Proposal[1]	Within-group consensus				Across-group consensus	Pattern (see Table 4.4)
	EU	PS	FD	AP		
Place records of general meetings on web	Yes	Yes	No	Yes	No	1
Disclose frequency of updating	Yes	Yes	Yes	Yes	No	1
Layer information	Yes	Yes	Yes	Yes	No	1
Maintain free search facility	Yes	Yes	Yes	Yes	No	1
Place audio-visual record of general meetings on web	Yes	Yes	No	Yes	No	1
Update website periodically, not continuously	Yes	No	Yes	Yes	Yes	2
Provide pre-packaged information	Yes	Yes	Yes	No	No	1
Webcast AGM	Yes	Yes	Yes	Yes	No	1
Disclose key information	No	No	No	No	No	3
Place minutes of one-to-one meetings on web	No	No	Yes	Yes	No	1/3
Broadcast general meetings	Yes	Yes	Yes	Yes	No	1
Replace AGM with online questioning	Yes	No	Yes	Yes	No	1

Note 1: Proposals are presented in the order shown in Table 4.2.

Four patterns of group consensus are possible, and these are set out in Table 4.4.

Table 4.4 Potential patterns of within-group and across-group consensus

Pattern	Likely conditions
Pattern 1: within-group consensus generally present; across-group consensus absent	Consequences of proposal* are clear, but impact differently upon the various interested parties
Pattern 2: within-group consensus generally present; across-group consensus present	Consequences of proposal* are clear, and impact similarly upon the various interested parties
Pattern 3: within-group consensus generally absent; across-group consensus absent	Proposal will impact differently upon the various interested parties, although the consequences of proposal* are uncertain
Pattern 4: within-group consensus generally absent; across-group consensus present	Consequences of proposal* are uncertain, although they are felt to impact similarly upon the various interested parties

* *'Consequences of proposal' refers to the identity and magnitude of the perceived costs and benefits to a particular group.*

The reason for distinguishing these different patterns is because the implications, especially for regulators, are very different. Where *within*-group consensus is generally absent, there would seem to be uncertainty regarding the true identity and/or magnitude of the costs and benefits to a specific group that shares a common interest. There is, therefore, clearly a need to investigate the costs and benefits further, so they become defined more clearly and their magnitude better evaluated. Where *across*-group consensus is absent, the outcome of a cost-benefit analysis would appear to differ depending on the nature of the group's interest, *i.e.* there is a conflict of interests. Where the issue is one that regulators feel should be addressed, there will be a need to resolve the conflict of interests, by regulating in favour of one particular group and/or seeking to mitigate the extent of the conflict.

Table 4.3 reveals that the most common dispersion pattern is pattern 1, *i.e.* within-group consensus generally present combined with across-group consensus absent. This indicates that the different groups broadly agree amongst themselves upon the desirability of the proposal, but that the groups hold quite distinct views. These different perspectives are reflected in the points raised by interviewees. Given this pattern, the appropriate policy response is to consider how to resolve the apparent conflict of interest, with the focus being on those proposals receiving strong support from at least one interested party

All respondents tend to agree that it is mildly desirable to update the website periodically, rather than continuously (pattern 2). Given this pattern, and the consensus that the proposal is desirable, the appropriate policy response is to consider introducing a mandatory requirement (or best practice guidelines). If the consensus had been that the proposal was *not* desirable, no regulatory action would have been called for.

By contrast, there is neither within-group, nor across-group consensus regarding the desirability of disclosing key information (pattern 3). In these circumstances, the appropriate policy response is to undertake further investigation to establish the nature and magnitude of the various perceived costs and benefits of the proposal to the various interested parties, prior to policy formulation

Table 4.5 summarises the main points raised by interviewees regarding the proposals. Only advantages are identified for those proposals receiving, on average, strong support. For the other proposals, as would be expected, there tends to be a mix of perceived advantages and disadvantages.

Table 4.5 Main points raised by interviewees regarding proposals

Proposal[1]	Advantages	Disadvantages
Place records of general meetings on web	Fairness	
Layer information	Communicative effectiveness Mitigate information overload Serve multiple audiences	
Place audio-visual record of general meetings on web	Fairness	Adverse impact on content and hence value of meetings
Update website periodically, not continuously	Supports efficient working practices	
Provide pre-packaged information		Cost to preparer Information equality across groups Over-regulation
Disclose key information	Usefulness Comparability	Commercial confidentiality
Place minutes of one-to-one meetings on web	Fairness	Adverse impact on content and hence value of meetings
Replace AGM with online questioning	AGM ineffective Value of two-way dialogue	Loss of control mechanism AGM useful source of information De-humanising

Note 1: Four of the proposals deemed less critical were not specifically discussed during interview: disclose frequency of updating, maintain free search facility, webcast AGM, and broadcast general meetings.

Finally, it was found that more frequent Internet users tended to favour many of the ICAS proposals to a significantly greater extent than those less familiar with the Internet. Bearing in mind that the ICAS proposals considered in this report are those that exploit the potential of the Internet to change business reporting practices, this finding is to be expected.

Endnote:

[10] The correlations are based on the non-parametric (Spearman) correlation coefficient. To calculate these correlations, Internet usage is coded on a 1 to 4 scale, where 'never' is coded 1 and 'almost daily' is coded 4.

CHAPTER FIVE

USEFULNESS OF NAVIGATION AIDS, SEARCH AIDS AND FILE FORMATS

Chapter two discussed the FASB *Fauxcom* project, as well as the surveys of web-reporting practices. These studies suggest a variety of desirable features of web-reporting. This chapter reports on the views of users, preparers and auditors regarding the usefulness of these features. For all features considered in this chapter, the response scale used was 1 (very useful); 2 (useful); 3 (fairly useful); 4 (of little use) and 5 (not useful at all). A final section investigates the relationship between respondents' familiarity with the Internet and their stated views.

Global navigation aids

Clearly it is important that business reporting information can be located easily on the company website. In particular, the practice of indexing financial information on the home page is considered by Ashbaugh *et al.* (1999, p251) to improve the usefulness of disclosures. Figure 5.1 reproduces the specific question asked and graphs the distribution of respondents' views; the mean and dispersion are shown in a panel on the right hand side of the graph.

Figure 5.1 Index business reporting information on home page

Question: Business reporting information is clearly indexed on the home page (*e.g.* titled Investor Relations) and not buried (*e.g.* under company history).

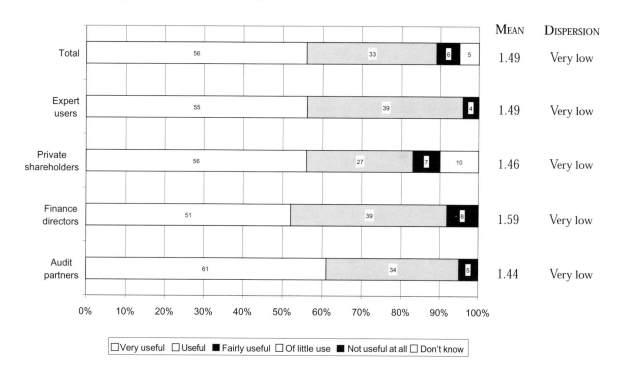

The groups display very similar responses to this question and the differences between the groups' views are not significant. This feature is considered by respondents to fall approximately mid-way between 'useful' and 'very useful' (overall mean = 1.49) and is the feature ranked by all groups as most useful out of all those considered in this chapter. Dispersion is very low for all groups.

The existence of a hyperlinked table of contents for the business reporting package (question 2) is identified as a useful navigation aid by FASB (2000, p23). FASB report that 71% of the US sites surveyed included this feature. Figure 5.2 presents the views of respondents.

Figure 5.2 Hyperlinked site map or table of contents available

Question: A hyperlinked site map or table of contents is available that shows all the major components in the business reporting package (hyperlinks allow the user to jump directly from one section to another, the link being activated by mouse-clicking on the source point).

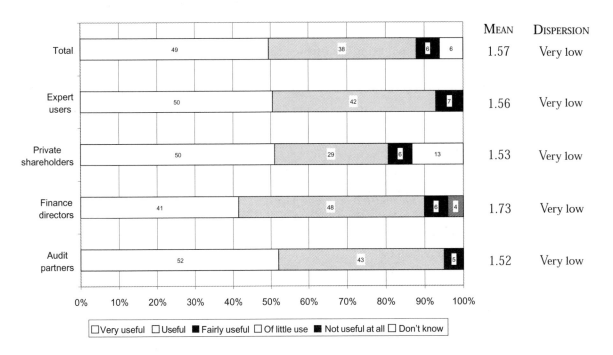

Once again, dispersion is very low for all groups and the differences between the groups' views are not significant. This feature is ranked as either the second or third most useful feature by all main groups (overall mean 1.57).

For the most part, interviewees discussed navigation aids quite generally. Several commented on the awkwardness of using on-screen reports and said that they used them only if they were in urgent need of seeing the report and accounts and did not have a printed copy to hand:

Something happens and you suddenly realise that you haven't got the most recent report and accounts ... so I go into their website ... sometimes it is a little bit difficult to navigate round, I must say. It's not quite as easy as reading a full set of report and accounts, where you've got everything in front of you, rather than just snippets on a screen. (expert user)

I do look at reports and accounts off the web, though my natural inclination is to find a hard copy because it's very difficult to read information on the screen. If somebody's unexpectedly coming you have to print it off, but it's a hundred pages long and that's a lot of printing; it's still not very user friendly. (expert user)

One preparer seemed aware of these problems:

Having got the information up there ... we're well into thinking of ways that we can make the information more accessible. (finance director)

Value of hyperlinks

Hyperlinks allow the user to jump directly from one section of a website to another (or indeed to jump to a completely different website). The hyperlink, normally highlighted in blue, is activated by mouse clicking on this source point. Having hyperlinked from the source point to the destination, it is common to find another link that allows the user to jump back to the original source. The *FauxCom* demonstration site (FASB, 1998) incorporates a number of these 'jump gates'. In particular, there are links between items in the financial statements ('the heart of the business report') and *(i)* the relevant note to the accounts, *(ii)* the relevant section of the Operating and Financial Review (OFR), and *(iii)* the five-year summary[11]. In addition, it also provides links between the OFR and the notes and, because the website seeks to combine the best of current practice in Internet distribution with the comprehensive reporting package envisioned by the AICPA (1994), between the OFR and relevant forward-looking information and relevant company background.

The importance of hyperlinks is endorsed by Ashbaugh *et al.* (1999). An experimental study conducted by Hodge (2001), indicates that firms can influence financial report users' perceptions by hyperlinking unaudited information to information in their audited financial statements. It was found that this influence is attenuated by attaching a simple 'audited/not audited' label.

The value of hyperlinks between different sections of the business reporting package was addressed in the present study by two multi-part questions. Table 5.1 presents summary data of the mean and dispersion for each group and the combined groups, while Figure 5.3 gives a visual representation of the overall ranking of their usefulness by all respondents.

Table 5.1 Usefulness of hyperlinks

Hyperlink	Mean responses (dispersion)				
	Total	Expert User	Private Shareholder	Finance Director	Audit Partner
Financial statements – note to accounts	1.66 Very low	1.53 Very low	1.67 Very low	1.84 Very low	1.74 Very low
Financial statements – OFR	1.86 Very low	1.80 Very low	1.86 Very low	2.11 Low	1.72 Very low
Financial statements – 5-year summary	2.12 Low	2.17 Low	1.91 Low	2.31 Moderate	2.37 Moderate
Note to accounts – OFR	2.16 Low	2.15 Low	2.13 Low	2.41 Low	1.98 Low
OFR – relevant forward-looking information	2.13 Low	2.11 Low	2.07 Low	2.44 Low	1.93 Very low
OFR – relevant company background	2.30 Low	2.32 Low	2.22 Low	2.54 Moderate	2.20 Low

Figure 5.3 Overall ranking of usefulness of hyperlinks between different sections of the business reporting package

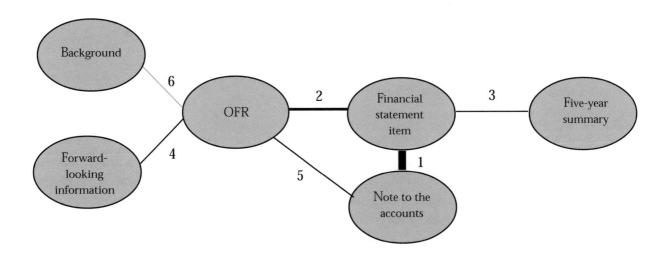

<u>Note:</u> The number shown alongside the link (and the thickness of the line) indicates the combined respondent groups' ranking of the link's usefulness.

The most useful link is considered to be that between the financial statement line item and the individual note to the accounts, followed by the financial statement line item and the relevant section of the OFR. The next three links have very similar means: between the financial statement line item and the five-year summary; the OFR and relevant forward-looking information; and the individual notes to the accounts and relevant sections of the OFR. The least useful link (although even this is considered moderately useful with a mean of 2.3) is that between the OFR and relevant company background.

The differences between the groups with regard to the top four ranked links are significant at the 5% level. Looking at the figures in Table 5.1, it can be seen that both expert users and audit partners rank the link between the financial statement line item and the five-year summary relatively low compared to the other two groups (ranked 5th and 6th respectively). They also rank the link between the OFR and relevant forward-looking information relatively more highly (ranked 3rd by both).

During the interviews, the only theme to emerge was in relation to the relatively lower usefulness of a link between the financial statements and the five-year summary. This was explained in terms of companies' rapid rate of change rendering such a long time frame unhelpful or even misleading:

To the professional user a five-year look back is just too long. If you'd put two, maybe three years then I might have marked it more positively. I mean, companies have changed such a lot in five years that it's just not relevant. (expert user)

It's only useful if the business hasn't changed in that five years. You can't restate for an acquisition, for example. It gets very, very subjective and so you end up needing tons of footnotes and I have found from time to time five-year summaries to be quite misleading. (expert user)

Ability to create graphs of data series

The *FauxCom* site also provides a wealth of graphic information – by 'pointing and clicking' on financial items it is possible to get a time series graph of the item. Figure 5.4 presents respondents' views of the usefulness of this feature.

Figure 5.4 Point and click graph facility

Question: The facility to 'point and click' on financial items to get a time series graph of the item.

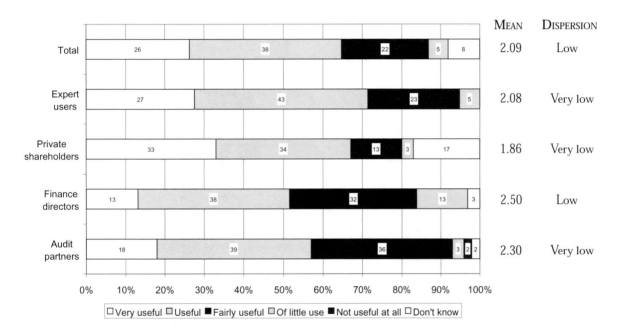

The differences between the groups' views are highly significant (0.1% level). It seems that users (especially the private shareholder group) rate this feature more highly than the other groups (especially finance directors) – the mean response for both user groups is within the 'useful' range, while those of finance directors and audit partners fall within the 'moderately useful' range. Within group dispersion is either low or very low.

Next and previous buttons

The provision of 'next' and 'previous' buttons on each web page allows users to move through the report in a linear fashion in the same way as the paper-based annual report. FASB (2000, p24) reports that 42% of the US sites surveyed included this feature. Figure 5.5 presents the views of the survey respondents.

Figure 5.5 Next and previous buttons

Question: 'Next' and 'previous' buttons at the bottom of the page.

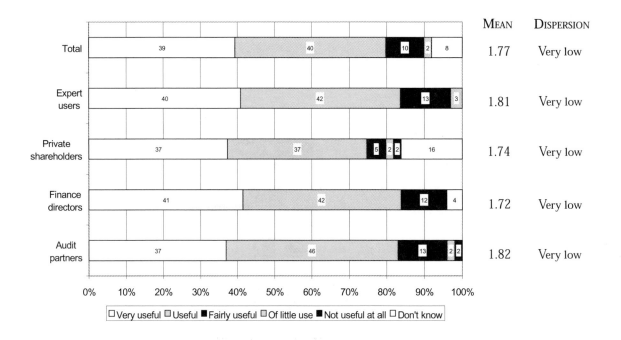

All four groups rank this feature fairly highly. The differences between the groups' views are not significant and within-group dispersion is in all cases very low.

Email alerts

The facility to sign up for email alerts (to receive press releases and other updates *via* email or notification that new information is posted on the web) is identified as a notable practice by FASB (2000, p13). Figure 5.6 presents the views of the survey respondents.

Figure 5.6 Email alerts

Question: Users can sign up for email alerts, to receive press releases and other updates *via* email or notification that new information is posted on the web

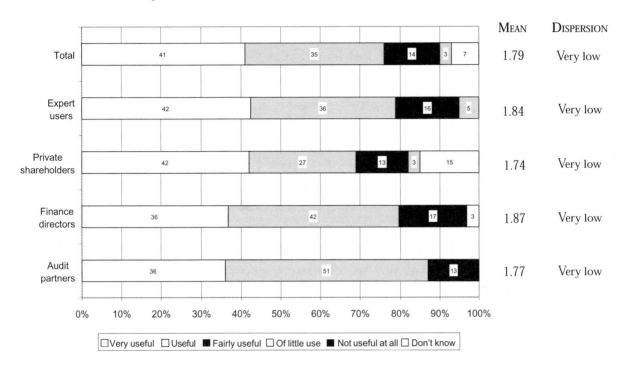

As in the case of next and previous buttons, all four groups rank this feature fairly highly. The differences between the groups' views are not significant and within-group dispersion is in all cases very low. One interviewee commented:

> *It comes back to this continuous issue ... What I see this doing is the ability to get away from the profit warnings ... If you get more drip-feed information it takes out the overreactions in the market place and that can only be good news. These days there are decent enough search engines that filter out the emails that you want to see.* (audit partner)

Arthur Andersen (2001) report that 45% of the top 250 FTSE companies include an email alert facility on their website.

File formats

It is apparent from surveys of company practice that the websites of even the best companies generally provide only one or two file formats. Yet the provision of multiple formats is, arguably, highly desirable, given the variety of contexts in which information is used. This study asked about the usefulness of five different formats and the summary results are shown in Table 5.2.

Table 5.2 Usefulness of file formats

File format	Mean responses (dispersion)				
	Total	Expert User	Private Shareholder	Finance Director	Audit Partner
HTML	2.50 Moderate	2.68 Moderate	2.30 Moderate	2.51 Low	2.55 Very low
PDF	2.51 Low	2.32 Low	2.66 High	2.46 Very low	2.65 Very low
Word-processed	2.31 Low	2.24 Low	2.31 Moderate	2.43 Low	2.37 Very low
Spreadsheet	2.21 Moderate	1.92 Very low	2.31 High	2.44 Moderate	2.36 Low
XBRL	2.41 Moderate	2.20 Low	2.61 High	2.46 Moderate	2.30 Very low

It should be noted that the 'don't know' category was quite large for these questions, especially for users and for the XBRL format. Based on those who did feel able to offer a view, each of the formats is seen as being at least 'fairly useful' by all groups (*i.e.* means<3.0). Overall, the spreadsheet format is seen as being of most use, followed by word-processed files and the XBRL format. The more common current formats (HTML and PDF) trail slightly behind in the rankings.

There are, however, distinct differences in the rankings of the groups. expert users rank the spreadsheet format top and HTML last. Private shareholders, by contrast, rank HTML top. Finance directors do not appear to make a significant distinction between the five formats, while audit partners rate PDF significantly below the rest.

The differences between groups are significant except for the word-processed format. Looking at the group means, it is clear that:

- private shareholders rank HTML relatively more highly than the other groups;
- private shareholders and audit partners rank PDF relatively less useful than the other groups;
- expert users rank the spreadsheet format relatively more highly than the other groups; and
- expert users and audit partners rank XBRL relatively more highly than the other groups.

The level of within-group dispersion is very variable, reflecting the groups varying levels of familiarity with the different formats. Private shareholders display either moderate or high dispersion for the five formats; at the other extreme, audit partners display either low or very low dispersion.

The final question asks about the usefulness of the principal feature of XBRL – its use of type tags that allow automatic inter-company comparisons. These tags provide information about information, *i.e.* 'meta-information' (Elliott, 2001). Figure 5.7 presents the results.

Figure 5.7 Type tags facilitate automatic comparisons

Question: XBRL incorporates type tags that hook information together, allowing one company to be compared to others automatically.

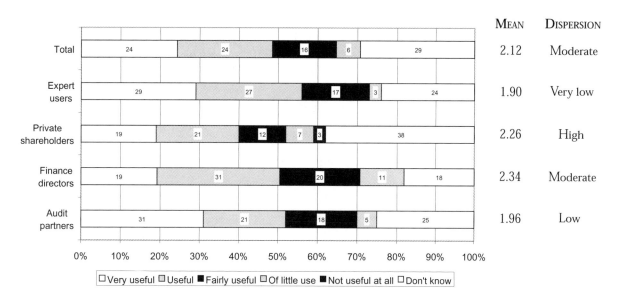

Once again, there is a high proportion of 'don't know' responses. Of those offering an opinion, group views differ significantly (at the 1% level). Expert users and audit partners appear to rate this feature more highly than the other two groups. It is interesting (and somewhat surprising) that finance directors are the group that rates this feature lowest. Perhaps some preparers are not looking forward to users routinely making explicit comparisons between 'their' company and others?

In commenting on the usefulness of alternative file formats, several interviewees remarked on the dangers of information being tampered with:

When we do new transactions there is a definite trend appearing where people are sending out the information memoranda on secure websites. The resistance that you will run into is that companies will see any procedure which accelerates [information dissemination] *in a format that they might not have complete control over as dangerous, because somebody might sneak in and feed some information in.* (expert user)

There are people out there in the market at the moment with financial information in a format that can be easily manipulated... At the end of the day, you can't substitute for actually extracting those numbers yourself and understanding what is behind the actual output. You know the composition of the numbers. Unless you understand what figures you put in to make the formulas, it is difficult to do a straight comparison or outputs ... Though it certainly would save a bit of time. (expert user)

We are very nervous about companies effectively using reports produced by us and sort of playing around with them to change them to a different presentation to make the point they want to make. (audit partner)

Others, especially expert users, felt strongly that the speed and ease of data transfer was very important:

If it's presented in something that I can easily import and I can easily then manipulate and store, then that's the best. (expert user)

That will make life much easier. (expert user)

We certainly do manipulate the information in other forms. If it is transportable so much the better. (expert user)

If you ask most companies can they send you the document in a readable form then they will do it if they trust you. As far as I'm concerned that's the best form for me – that speeds it up. (expert user)

One private shareholder who said that he had been in the software business for a long time and who preferred PDF format, observed:

It can't be corrupted accidentally by other people. Word is diabolical because Word comes out differently depending on how you've got your PC configured. Excel is slightly better. (private shareholder)

It was apparent from the interviewees' comments that (as of June/July 2000 when the questionnaire was completed) very few individuals had more than a hazy knowledge of XBRL. Some were very skeptical:

It comes down to the quality of the programming in the first place. (audit partner)

I'm deeply skeptical about automatic links…there is a danger that you lose judgement…by definition what you are doing is substituting someone else's judgement for the user's judgement as to what is comparable. (audit partner)

Others were very positive:

The easier that we can make it to pick up the data, exchange it and analyse it the more useful it is going to be. If we are going to put all the effort into getting it up there on the web then if we can do it against the standard that allows the analysts all over the world to pick up the data using common terminology that is derived from common standards then it's got to make sense. (finance director)

Anything that helps me to do the job quicker and generate greater analytical ability is a positive for me. (expert user)

To be able to compare companies automatically must be a big advantage and would do away with some of the dross, if it were truly comparable information. (expert user)

What we are really talking here is about the development of standards by which information can be presented or accessed and we have no problem at all in understanding why that's desirable and helpful. (finance director)

Impact of familiarity with the Internet

Perhaps surprisingly, the correlations between frequency of Internet use (see Figure 4.1 above) and the usefulness of navigation and search aids were not generally very high. More frequent Internet users were statistically more likely to believe that four features, in particular, were useful: index on home page; hyperlinked site map or table of contents; hyperlinks between the financial statements and the notes; and email alerts[12].

The responses to four questions regarding file formats were significantly negatively correlated with frequency of Internet use.[13]. This shows, not surprisingly, that more frequent Internet users were statistically more likely to believe that four formats, in particular, were useful: PDF; word processed; spreadsheet; and XBRL.

Overview and summary of key points

As in chapter four, to serve as a basis for summarising the key points to emerge from the findings presented in this chapter, three tables have been prepared. Table 5.3 presents, in descending order of usefulness, the combined mean response to the seventeen features.

Table 5.3 Combined mean response to the suggested web features

Feature	Mean response[1]	Descriptive label
Index business reporting information on home page	1.49	Extremely useful
Hyperlinked site map or table of contents available	1.57	
Hyperlinks between financial statements and notes	1.66	
Next and previous buttons	1.77	Useful
Email alerts	1.79	
Hyperlinks between financial statements and OFR	1.86	
Point and click graph facility	2.09	
Hyperlinks between financial statements and 5-year summary	2.12	
Type tags facilitate automatic comparisons	2.12	
Hyperlinks between OFR and forward-looking information	2.13	
Hyperlinks between notes and OFR	2.16	
Spreadsheet format	2.21	
Hyperlinks between OFR and company background	2.30	
Word-processed format	2.31	Moderately useful
XBRL format	2.41	
HTML format	2.50	
PDF format	2.51	

Note 1: Mean responses are shown in descending order of agreement.

The general pattern of results across groups and questions is very consistent, in that all groups consider all features to be, on average, at least moderately useful:

- three features are considered, on average, *extremely useful* (index business reporting information on home page, hyperlinked site map or table of contents available, and hyperlinks between financial statements and notes);
- ten features are considered, on average, *useful* (next and previous buttons, email alerts, hyperlinks between financial statements and OFR, point and click graph facility, hyperlinks between financial statements and 5-year summary, type tags facilitate automatic comparisons, hyperlinks between OFR and forward-looking information, hyperlinks between notes and OFR, spreadsheet format, and hyperlinks between OFR and company background); and
- four features are considered, on average, *moderately useful* (word processed, XBRL, HTML and PDF formats).

Table 5.4 focuses on the level of within-group and across-group consensus, on the same basis that was established at the end of chapter four. In this chapter, the scale is one-sided (not useful to extremely useful) and so a lack of across-group consensus does not indicate a conflict of interests in the same way as the two-sided agree-disagree scale used in chapter four. There is clearly a mix of pattern 1 and pattern 2.

Pattern 1 (within-group consensus generally present; across-group consensus absent) is likely to occur where particular groups view the perceived usefulness of the feature similarly, but the perception varies across the various interested parties. The appropriate policy response might reasonably depend on how highly users rated the feature. If users rate the feature highly, policy makers should consider *requiring* preparers to incorporate the feature on their website (unless preparers can establish any significant barriers to this). However, if users do *not* rate the feature highly, policy makers should merely *encourage* preparers to incorporate the feature on their website.

Pattern 2 (within-group consensus generally present; across-group consensus present) is likely to occur where the perceived usefulness of the feature is viewed in a similar manner by all. In this case, the appropriate policy response might reasonably depend on how highly all groups rated the feature. If rated highly, policy makers should consider *requiring* preparers to incorporate the feature on their website. However, if the feature is *not* rated highly, policy makers should merely *encourage* preparers to incorporate the feature on their website.

The general level of within-group consensus is high: across the 17 questions asked and the four respondent groups 50% of dispersion measures were 'very low' and a further 31% were 'low'. Table 5.5 summarises the main points raised by interviewees regarding the features.

Table 5.4 Patterns of within-group and across-group consensus observed

Feature[1]	Within-group consensus				Across-group consensus	Pattern
	EU	PS	FD	AP		
Index business reporting information on home page	Yes	Yes	Yes	Yes	Yes	2
Hyperlinked site map or table of contents available	Yes	Yes	Yes	Yes	Yes	2
Hyperlinks between financial statements and notes	Yes	Yes	Yes	Yes	No	1
Next and previous buttons	Yes	Yes	Yes	Yes	Yes	2
Email alerts	Yes	Yes	Yes	Yes	Yes	2
Hyperlinks between financial statements and OFR	Yes	Yes	Yes	Yes	No	1
Point and click graph facility	Yes	Yes	Yes	Yes	No	1
Hyperlinks between financial statements and 5-year summary	Yes	Yes	Yes	Yes	No	1
Type tags facilitate automatic comparisons	Yes	No	Yes	Yes	No	1
Hyperlinks between OFR and forward-looking information	Yes	Yes	Yes	Yes	No	1
Hyperlinks between notes and OFR	Yes	Yes	Yes	Yes	Yes	2
Spreadsheet format	Yes	No	Yes	Yes	No	1
Hyperlinks between OFR and company background	Yes	Yes	Yes	Yes	Yes	2
Word-processed format	Yes	Yes	Yes	Yes	Yes	2
XBRL format	Yes	No	Yes	Yes	No	1
HTML format	Yes	Yes	Yes	Yes	No	1
PDF format	Yes	No	Yes	Yes	No	1

Note 1: Features are presented in the order shown in Table 5.3

Table 5.5 Main points raised by interviewees regarding features

Feature	Advantages	Disadvantages
Navigation aids	Helps overcome awkwardness of using on-screen reports	
Hyperlinks between financial statements and 5-year summary		Rapid change renders summary unhelpful or misleading
Email alerts	Drip feed helps overcome market over-reactions	
Downloadable/cut and paste file formats	Speed and ease of data transfer	Dangers of information being tampered with
XBRL and type tags	Aids comparisons	Integrity of comparisons

Finally, more frequent Internet users were statistically more likely to believe that four features (index on home page; hyperlinked site map or table of contents; hyperlinks between the financial statements and the notes; and email alerts) and four formats (PDF, word processed, spreadsheet, and XBRL) were useful.

Endnotes:

[11] The OFR is known as the MD&A in the US.

[12] Based on associations at, at least, the 5% level.

[13] Based on associations at, at least, the 10% level.

CHAPTER SIX

GROUP PROFILES

In chapters four and five, questions have been examined one at a time, establishing and then comparing and contrasting the views of the four groups. Additional insights can emerge by reviewing each group's set of responses. This complementary perspective allows a better appreciation of the characteristic mind set for each group. In other words, it provides a 'profile' of each group. In this chapter, group profiles are presented and discussed. Two profiles are presented for each group, one covering the ICAS (1999) proposals, the other dealing with the perceived usefulness of various web-reporting features.

Group profiles for the ICAS (1999) proposals

Panels A to D set out each group's level of agreement with the ICAS proposals, based on the observed group mean. The descriptive labels used are those set out in chapter one (p5).

Panel A Summary of expert users' views of ICAS proposals

Strong agreement
   Layer information
   Place records of general meetings on web
   Disclose frequency of website updating

Reasonably strong agreement
   Disclose key information
   Maintain free search facility
   Place audio-visual of general meetings on web
   Webcast AGM

Mild agreement
   Provide pre-packaged information
   Update website information periodically, not continuously

Neutral
   Broadcast general meetings

Mild disagreement
   Place minutes of one-to-one meetings on web
   Replace AGM with online questioning

Panel B Summary of private shareholders' views of ICAS proposals

Strong agreement
    Layer information
    Place records of general meetings on web
    Disclose frequency of website updating

Reasonably strong agreement
    Disclose key information
    Maintain free search facility
    Provide pre-packaged information
    Place audio-visual of general meetings on web
    Webcast AGM

Mild agreement
    Place minutes of one-to-one meetings on web
    Update website information periodically, not continuously

Neutral
    Broadcast general meetings

Reasonably strong disagreement
    Replace AGM with online questioning

Comparing Panels A and B, the two user groups, it is readily apparent that the profiles are very similar. On average, they agree, to a greater or lesser extent, with the vast majority of the ICAS proposals. The only proposal with which both user groups disagree is the proposal to replace the AGM with online questioning expert, users also disagree with the proposal to place minutes of one-to-one meetings on the web (by contrast, private shareholders mildly agree). The only other difference between the two groups relates to the provision of pre-packaged information. Private shareholders agree more strongly with this than expert users.

Panel C Summary of finance directors' views of ICAS proposals

Strong agreement

–

Reasonably strong agreement
Layer information
Disclose frequency of website updating

Mild agreement
Place records of general meetings on web
Update website information periodically, not continuously

Neutral
Maintain free search facility
Provide pre-packaged information
Place audio-visual of general meetings on web

Mild disagreement
Disclose key information
Webcast AGM
Replace AGM with online questioning

Reasonably strong disagreement
Broadcast general meetings

Strong disagreement
Place minutes of one-to-one meetings on web

It is interesting to next compare the views of users with preparers (Panel C). This discussion focuses on comparing expert users with finance directors. (Given the close similarity between the user groups, there is little point in repeating the exercise for private shareholders as well.) The first thing to note about the finance director profile is the greater balance between agreement and disagreement with the proposals. In fact, finance directors are, on average, negative about five proposals and positive about only four.

Finance director views fall into a different descriptive category than expert user views for ten of the twelve proposals. In all cases, finance directors' level of agreement is below that of expert users. In two cases, the difference is particularly great: while expert users and private shareholders are reasonably strongly in agreement with the proposals to disclose key information and to webcast the AGM, finance directors are in mild disagreement (*i.e.* three categories of difference).

Panel D Summary of audit partners' views of ICAS proposals

> *Strong agreement*
>   Place records of general meetings on web
>   Disclose frequency of website updating
>
> *Reasonably strong agreement*
>   Layer information
>   Update website information periodically, not continuously
>
> *Mild agreement*
>   Maintain free search facility
>   Place audio-visual of general meetings on web
>   Webcast AGM
>
> *Neutral*
>   Disclose key information
>   Provide pre-packaged information
>   Place minutes of one-to-one meetings on web
>
> *Mild disagreement*
>   Broadcast general meetings
>   Replace AGM with online questioning

Next the views of expert users with audit partners (Panel D) are compared. Audit partner views are more closely aligned to those of expert users. Audit partners offer a degree of support for seven of the ICAS proposals and are against only two. With the exception of one proposal, there is no more than one category of difference between the average views of these two groups. In six cases, expert users' level of agreement is one category stronger than audit partners, while in two cases expert users' level of agreement is one category *less* strong (audit partners are more concerned that website information be updated periodically rather than continuously and less against placing minutes of one-to-one meetings on the web). Audit partners are, however, much less concerned that key information be disclosed.

Finally, a comparison between finance directors' views and audit partners' views reveals that audit partners are more supportive of the ICAS proposals that finance directors. This is especially the case for minutes of one-to-one meetings, where there is a difference of three descriptive categories.

The picture that emerges from these profiles and the comparisons between them is that users are generally supportive of the ICAS proposals, preparers are moderately opposed to a significant number, while auditors fall somewhere in between. The auditors' position reflects the complex and sometimes conflicting array of motivations and concerns to which auditors are subject. These act to pull auditors in different directions: professional public interest concerns result in an identification with the user perspective; the desire to support the 'client' company results in an identification with the preparer perspective; and self-interest can result in a unique auditor perspective.

There are three proposals that appear to have little support across the groups: the broadcast of general meetings; the placing of minutes of one-to-one meetings on the web; and the replacement of the AGM with online questioning.

Group profiles for web-reporting features

Panels E to H set out each group's view of the perceived usefulness of various web-reporting features, based on the observed group mean. The descriptive labels used are those set out in chapter one, page five.

Panel E Summary of expert users' views of web features

Extremely useful
Indexed on home page
Hyperlinked table of contents
Hyperlinks financial statements/notes

Useful
Hyperlinks financial statements/OFR
Hyperlinks financial statements/5-year summary
Hyperlinks notes/OFR
Hyperlinks OFR/forward-looking
Point and click graph facility
Next and previous buttons
Email alerts
Word-processed format
Spreadsheet format
XBRL format
Type tags facilitate automatic comparisons

Moderately useful
Hyperlinks OFR/background
HTML format
PDF format

Panel F Summary of private shareholders' views of web features

Extremely useful
  Indexed on home page
  Hyperlinked table of contents
  Hyperlinks financial statements/notes

Useful
  Hyperlinks financial statements/OFR
  Hyperlinks financial statements/5-year summary
  Hyperlinks notes/OFR
  Hyperlinks OFR/forward-looking
  Hyperlinks OFR/background
  Point and click graph facility
  Next and previous buttons
  Email alerts
  HTML format
  Type tags facilitate automatic comparisons

Moderately useful
  PDF format
  Word-processed format
  Spreadsheet format
  XBRL format

Looking first at the views of users (Panels E and F), it is immediately clear that *all* of the features listed are found to be useful by both professional and non-professional users, although the degree of usefulness varies across the features. For both groups, a few features are deemed 'extremely useful', while a few are merely 'moderately useful', with the majority falling into the middle range. There are very few differences between the views of the two user groups. Both agree that effective global navigation aids and also that hyperlinking *within* the audited section of the annual report and accounts (*i.e.* between the financial statements and the relevant notes to the accounts) are extremely useful. For other features, differences relate in the main to the relative usefulness of various file formats.

Panel G Summary of finance directors' views of web features

Extremely useful
Indexed on home page

Useful
Hyperlinked table of contents
Hyperlinks financial statements/notes
Hyperlinks financial statements/OFR
Next and previous buttons
Email alerts

Moderately useful
Hyperlinks financial statements/5-year summary
Hyperlinks notes/OFR
Hyperlinks OFR/forward-looking
Hyperlinks OFR/background
Point and click graph facility
HTML format
PDF format
Word-processed format
Spreadsheet format
XBRL format
Type tags facilitate automatic comparisons

Once again, because of the remarkable similarity of views between the two user groups, user and preparer views are compared only in terms of the expert user group. Finance directors rate as extremely useful only one feature (indexing on home page) and only a further five as useful. Thus, preparers generally rate the usefulness of features below users; this is the case for eight features, all rated one descriptive category lower by finance directors. The three features rated only moderately useful by expert users are rated likewise by preparers.

Panel H Summary of audit partners' views of web features

Extremely useful
   Indexed on home page
   Hyperlinked table of contents

Useful
   Hyperlinks financial statements/notes
   Hyperlinks financial statements/OFR
   Hyperlinks notes/OFR
   Hyperlinks OFR/forward-looking
   Hyperlinks OFR/background
   Point and click graph facility
   Next and previous buttons
   Email alerts
   XBRL format
   Type tags facilitate automatic comparisons

Moderately useful
   Hyperlinks financial statements/5-year summary
   HTML format
   PDF format
   Word-processed format
   Spreadsheet format

Panel H profiles the views of audit partners. Their views are very similar to those of users, both in the overall usefulness of the package of features and in relation to specific features. Audit partners rate only four features in a descriptive category below expert users and one feature (hyperlinks between OFR and relevant company background) they consider more useful.

Given the marked differences between the views of users and preparers, and the marked similarity of views between users and auditors, it follows that there are marked differences between the views of finance directors and audit partners. Finance directors rate seven features one descriptive category lower than audit partners.

Summary of key points

In this chapter, the views of each respondent group in relation to a set of questions (first the set of ICAS web-reporting proposals and, second, the set of potentially useful web-reporting features) are brought together. This facilitates the comparison of each group's views across questions and with the profiles of other groups.

In relation to the ICAS (1999) proposals, both user groups agree (on average) with the majority of the proposals. Replacing the AGM with online questioning finds favour with neither group while the provision of minutes of one-to-one meetings is rejected by expert users. By contrast, preparers favour very few of the proposals (arguably only the less radical ones). Auditors fall in between, tending more towards the users' views than the preparers' views. These findings indicate the existence of important conflicts of interest between the groups. The implications of these differences for policy making are considered in chapter seven.

In relation to the web-reporting features, the differences are much less pronounced. All features are considered by all groups to be, at least, moderately useful (*i.e.* group mean < 2.7). However, the majority of features are considered by both user groups and auditors to be extremely useful (group mean < 1.7) or useful (group mean between 1.7 and 2.3), whereas preparers consider the majority of features only moderately useful (*i.e.* group mean between 2.3 and 2.7). This suggests that preparers systematically *underestimate* the perceived usefulness of web-reporting features to users. Implications are discussed in chapter seven.

CHAPTER SEVEN

CONCLUSIONS AND RECOMMENDATIONS

This chapter summarises and discusses the main findings to arise from this study. The three areas of the study are considered in turn:

- company reporting obligations;
- attitudes to ICAS (1999) proposals re web-reporting; and
- usefulness of navigation aids, search aids and file formats.

It then considers the implications of these findings for preparers and policy makers. A number of tentative recommendations follow.

Company reporting obligations

There was a very high level of agreement regarding the reporting obligations that a listed company has in relation to various stakeholder groups. Existing investors were given highest priority, with 84% of the respondents rating the obligation as 'absolute'. Potential investors and employees also ranked highly, with 73% of the respondents rating the obligation to potential investors as 'major' or 'absolute', while the figure for employees was 63%. The interview evidence suggested that employees were rated highly because of the importance of intellectual capital to many businesses and their increasing role in corporate governance. The other three groups (community/public, suppliers and customers) rated less highly, but nevertheless significantly.

These findings indicate that all six groups are considered to be legitimate user groups, in the sense that they have a moral right to receive information of relevance to them. To date, however, the regulatory framework has focused on the needs of shareholders. There is clearly a need for research to establish whether the other stakeholder groups have specialist information needs and, if so, exactly what they are. The findings of this study suggest that corporate reporting practices should develop to satisfy any additional information needs.

On average, private shareholders agreed strongly with the principle that private shareholders should be consulted on issues to do with company external reporting whereas the level of agreement of other respondent groups was mild. (Note that the question addressed the principle of consultation and did not specify the identity of the consulting body.) The vast majority of private shareholders either agreed strongly or agreed, whereas the vast majority in the other groups either agreed or were neutral. Given that no interested party appeared to oppose this principle, and some parties were strongly supportive, the inference must be that, despite the lack of interest and understanding sometimes attributable to members of this group, its views should not be ignored in the development of business reporting.

In combination, these findings are consistent with a more inclusive approach to corporate reporting that both consults and reports more widely than has historically been the case.

Attitudes to ICAS (1999) proposals re web reporting

All but three of the proposals received, on average, at least mild support from the combined group of 538 respondents. Support was strong for placing records of general meetings on the web, for disclosing the frequency of updating of web reporting and for layering information. By contrast, the combined group expressed, on average, neutrality or mild disagreement in relation to placing minutes of one-to-one meetings on the web, broadcasting general meetings and replacing the AGM with online questioning.

Importantly, however, the views held by the respondent groups differed significantly, due to the different motivations and perspectives of those groups. Preparers, in particular, supported very few of the proposals, yet both user groups agreed (often quite strongly) with the majority of the proposals, while auditors' views tended to fall in between. There were clearly conflicts of interest present.

The views of respondent groups in relation to the complete set of ICAS (1999) proposals can be summarised using the form of visual representation introduced by Cyert and Ijiri (1974) (see chapter two). This is done in Figure 7.1, where the relative areas of overlap depicted are based informally (*i.e.* not calculated mathematically) on the findings of this study. Specifically, the area of overlap between the views of users (the pooled groups of expert users and private shareholders) and preparers (area I + II) is less than the area of overlap between preparers and audit partners (area I + III), which in turn is less than the area of overlap between users and auditors (area I + IV). The latter area is less than the area of overlap between the views of expert users and private (non-professional) shareholders (area B).

Figure 7.1: Conflicts of interest in relation to ICAS (1999) proposals

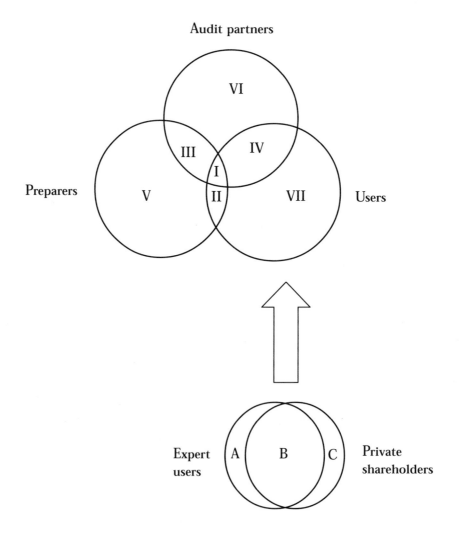

In general, the picture is one where audit partners' views fall between the views of users and preparers. This is perhaps to be expected. The audit partners are members of a professional body that has public interest responsibilities, and users (specifically, shareholders) are the auditors legal client, yet it is with the company that the auditor has the closest relationship. It is to be expected, therefore, that auditors will be more aware than users of the problems in implementing the proposed changes in business reporting. In addition, it is the company management and not the users who effectively (*i.e. de facto*) appoint and set the remuneration of the auditor. For this reason, auditors may feel obliged (consciously or sub-consciously) to lobby on behalf of the client company (Watts and Zimmerman, 1986, ch.13). It is also possible that auditors can also be expected to exhibit a degree of self interest, linked to the risks and returns available from the provision of auditing services.

In examining the individual proposals more closely, the analysis in chapter four examined not only the absolute level of agreement/disagreement of each group with the proposal, but also on the degree of within-group and across-group consensus. A lack of across-group consensus indicates the existence of conflict of interests. A lack of within-group consensus suggests that there is uncertainty regarding the true identity and/or magnitude of the costs and benefits to a specific group that shares a common interest. This calls for the costs and benefits to be investigated further, so they become defined more clearly and their magnitude better evaluated.

All but three of the proposals received, on average, at least mild support from the combined group, as follows:

- there was strong agreement with three proposals (placing records of general meetings on the web, disclosing the frequency of updating and layering information);
- there was reasonably strong support for two proposals (maintaining a free search facility and placing an audio-visual record of general meetings on the web);
- there was mild support for four proposals (updating website periodically, not continuously, providing pre-packaged information, webcasting the AGM and disclosing key management information);
- on average, respondents were neutral towards two proposals (placing minutes of one-to-one meetings on the web and broadcasting general meetings); and
- there was mild disagreement towards one proposal (replacing the AGM with online questioning).

The most commonly observed dispersion pattern was pattern 1, *i.e.* within-group consensus present but across-group consensus absent. In these circumstances, policy makers should consider how to resolve the apparent conflict of interest, with the focus being on those proposals receiving strong support from at least one interested party.

Once instance of pattern 2 (both across-group and within-group consensus present) was observed (update website periodically, not continuously) and this was combined with either mild or reasonably strong agreement from the four respondent groups. In this situation, where the consensus level of support is weak, policy makers could either consider introducing a mandatory requirement (or best practice guidelines) or take no further action.

Finally, there were two instances of pattern 3 (a lack of consensus both across groups and within groups). These occurred for the proposal to disclose key information (where the group responses ranged from mildly disagree to reasonably strongly agree) and the proposal to place minutes of one-to-one meetings on the web (where the mean group responses ranged from strongly disagree to mildly agree). In these cases, the policy response should be to undertake further investigation to establish the nature and magnitude of the various perceived costs and benefits of the proposal to the various interested parties prior to policy formulation.

It was found that those respondents who were more familiar with the Internet (*i.e.* more frequent users) expressed a stronger level of agreement with six proposals involving the extended use of the Internet for business reporting. It is, therefore, to be expected that as familiarity with the Internet increases among the user population, the strength of user agreement will also increase.

Usefulness of navigation aids, search aids and file formats

All respondent groups considered all features to be, on average, at least fairly useful (*i.e.* group means < 3). As a consequence, there were no real conflicts of interest, although there was in some cases significant disagreement over the degree of usefulness of the feature (*i.e.* a lack of across-group consensus). The combined group of 538 respondents considered three features, on average, extremely useful (index of business reporting information on home page, hyperlinked site map or table of contents available, and hyperlinks between financial statements and notes) and four features only moderately useful (word-processed, XBRL, HTML and PDF formats). The remainders were considered useful.

This set of questions produced a more evenly balanced number of pattern 1 (perceived usefulness of the feature is viewed similarly by particular groups, but the perception varies across the various interested parties) and pattern 2 (the perceived usefulness of the feature is viewed in a similar manner by all) consensus patterns. Preparers fairly consistently rated usefulness below users. This suggests that preparers consistently underestimate the usefulness of certain features to users and hence are less likely to incorporate them into corporate websites.

Given that all respondent groups considered all features to be, on average, at least fairly useful, there seems little reason for policy makers not to encourage preparers to incorporate these features on their websites. The supplementary interview evidence did, however, uncover some concerns regarding the use of different file formats and the level of usefulness of the five formats was seen by all groups as, on average, only 'moderately useful' (the exception being expert users who rated spreadsheets as 'useful'. This suggests that, in the case of file formats, further investigation is required into the risks associated with accidental corruption, tampering and bias.

Those respondents who were more familiar with the Internet considered four features to be significantly more useful than respondents who were less familiar with the Internet. Once again, it is, therefore, to be expected that as familiarity with the Internet increases among the user population, the perceived usefulness of these features will also increase.

Recommendations

Based on the findings of this study, and the foregoing discussion of these findings, the following eight general recommendations are made. In formulating these recommendations, account has been taken not only of the absolute response of each of the four key respondent groups to the question posed, but also the degree of within-group and across-group consensus, and also the issues raised during supplementary interviews.

Company reporting obligations

Recommendation 1: Corporate reporting practices should be developed (through the joint efforts of regulators, companies, the accountancy profession and academics) to satisfy the specialist needs of stakeholder groups other than existing shareholders.

Justification: All interested parties appear to accept that other stakeholder groups are legitimate user groups, to whom listed companies owe a reporting obligation.

Recommendation 2: Private shareholders should be consulted by those with a role in the development of corporate reporting practices (*i.e.* regulators, companies, the accountancy profession and academics) on issues to do with company external reporting. (Note that the other recommendations in this report accord equal status to the expressed views of private shareholders.)

Justification: All interested parties (especially private shareholders) expressed this view. It is widely recognised that users are not well represented in the policy-making process (for example, there is a general absence of written submissions by users to rule-making bodies). It is likely, therefore, that the views of user groups will have to be actively sought out.

Recommendation 3: Policy makers should consider requiring (or at least encouraging *via* best practice guidelines) the following five ICAS (1999) proposals:

- place records of general meetings on web
- disclose frequency of web updating
- layer information
- maintain free search facility
- place audio-visual record of general meetings on web.

Justification: On average, both user groups support these proposals strongly or reasonably strongly and preparers are at worst neutral. It seems clear, therefore, that the advantages of these proposals outweigh the disadvantages.

Recommendation 4: There should be no immediate moves made to encourage or require the following three ICAS (1999) proposals:

- place minutes of one-to-one meetings on web
- broadcast general meetings
- replace AGM with online questioning.

Justification: On average, *all* groups either disagree or are neutral towards these proposals (the minor exception is that private shareholders mildly agree that the minutes of one-to-one meetings be placed on the web). It seems clear, therefore, that the perceived disadvantages of these proposals currently outweigh the advantages.

Recommendation 5: Further research should be conducted to investigate the nature, magnitude and incidence of the costs and benefits relating to two ICAS (1999) proposals:

- disclose key information
- webcast AGM.

Justification: On average, these proposals receive reasonably strong support from both user groups, yet preparers are in mild disagreement. Thus, these changes are unlikely to be instigated by preparers and would require regulation. It is, therefore, critical that the costs and benefits are well understood before there is regulatory intervention. In particular, many commentators argue that the disclosure of key information used to manage the company is essential to the development of business reporting. Unfortunately, there are perceived to be major potential disadvantages to be set against the major potential advantages (in particular, the issue of commercial confidentiality). To what extent are expressed concerns about commercial confidentiality excuses, genuinely perceived threats (yet without significant substance) or actual threats?

Recommendation 6: Further research is desirable to investigate the nature, magnitude and incidence of the costs and benefits relating to two ICAS (1999) proposals:

- update website periodically, not continuously
- provide pre-packaged information.

Justification: On average, these proposals receive only mild support from both user groups (the exception is that private shareholders agree reasonably strongly that pre-packaged information be provided), and preparers are also mildly supportive or neutral. Thus, these proposals are perceived to have some potential advantages and no major disadvantages.

Recommendation 7: Best practice guidelines be introduced by those with a role in the development of corporate reporting practices (*i.e.* regulators, companies, the accountancy profession and academics) to encourage preparers to incorporate the following navigation and search aids into their websites:

- index of business reporting information on home page
- hyperlinked site map or table of contents
- hyperlinks between
    - financial statements and notes
    - financial statements and OFR
    - financial statements and five-year summary
    - notes and OFR
    - OFR and forward-looking information
- point and click graph facility
- next and previous buttons
- email alerts
- type tags to facilitate automatic comparisons.

Justification: Preparers are shown (in the absence of any concerns regarding the potential disadvantages of the features) to systematically *underestimate* the perceived usefulness of most features to users. On average, both user groups rate these features as either extremely useful or useful, while preparers and auditors rate them at least moderately useful. The likely advantages to users are, therefore, significant but, in the absence of some intervention, underprovision seems likely to occur.

Recommendation 8: Research should be conducted to investigate the validity of concerns that the provision of alternative file formats that can be manipulated will have adverse consequences.

Justification: The potential benefits of these formats are considerable in terms of the speed and ease of data transfer and analysis; however the risks associated with accidental corruption, tampering and bias demand careful consideration.

Concluding remarks

This study's findings with regard to company reporting obligations are consistent with a more inclusive approach to corporate reporting that both consults and reports more widely than has historically been the case. There was considerable variation in views among respondent groups regarding the ICAS (1999) proposals, with user groups being generally more supportive than both auditors and (especially) preparers. It is, therefore, likely that change will require regulatory intervention. The usefulness of various features of web-reporting were generally recognised by all respondent groups, although preparers placed lesser value on the features than users, suggesting that underprovision may occur in the absence of regulatory intervention. It is likely that views regarding many of the issues raised in this report will change gradually over time as familiarity with the Internet increases among the population. Those respondents who were more familiar with the Internet responded more positively to many questions than respondents who were less familiar with the Internet.

An important general conclusion to emerge from this study is that there is widespread support for changes that widen access (or ease of access) to information. Thus, there is support for those ICAS proposals that use web-reporting as a supplementary and augmenting mechanism (place record of general meetings on web, place audio-visual of general meetings on web; and webcast AGM) and those that ease access by restructuring of the information set (layering; free search; and prepackaging). There is also support for the use of technical web features that enhance the ease of access.

However by rejecting the proposal to replace the AGM with online questioning, respondents are rejecting the idea of *substituting* people-based communication with web-based communication. The proposals to 'broadcast AGMs' and 'place minutes of one-to-one meetings on the web', are also rejected however, despite being supplementary in nature. This may be attributable to the tension that appears to exist between the desire to widen access and the fear that, in so doing, the information quality of these people-based communications may be compromised (the expressed fear that the tenor of these meetings may change for the worse).

APPENDIX

EXTRACT FROM QUESTIONNAIRE

SECTION A

Reporting obligations

A1. In your view, what is the extent of a listed company's obligation to report to each of the following stakeholder groups?

	None	Slight	Moderate	Major	Absolute	Don't know
• Customers	1	2	3	4	5	dk
• Employees	1	2	3	4	5	dk
• Suppliers	1	2	3	4	5	dk
• Existing investors	1	2	3	4	5	dk
• Potential investors	1	2	3	4	5	dk
• Community/the public	1	2	3	4	5	dk

A2. To what extent do you agree that private shareholders should be consulted on issues to do with company external reporting?

Strongly agree	Agree	Neutral	Disagree	Strongly disagree	Don't know
1	2	3	4	5	dk

Internet-based information

It is now clear that business reporting will increasingly occur via the Internet. This technology allows much larger information sets to be made available although, to avoid information overload, these will need to be structured to facilitate easy navigation and search. The questions in this section relate only to information provided using the Internet *via* company websites. They are based upon recent reports by accounting standard-setting bodies and professional bodies.

A3. How often do you use the Internet?

Never ☐   Rarely ☐   About once weekly ☐   Almost daily ☐

A4. To what extent do you agree or disagree that companies should be required to do the following?

	Strongly agree	Agree	Neutral	Disagree	Strongly disagree	Don't know
Make available key information that it uses to manage the company (subject to legitimate concerns re commercial confidentiality and risk of misinterpretation)	1	2	3	4	5	dk
Layer information to avoid information overload, while providing the detail desired by many (i.e. overview in top layer, becoming progressively more complex and detailed in lower layers)	1	2	3	4	5	dk
Provide a range of pre-packaged information, based on a standardised template for each group of users, specified by an external regulatory body. (The template gives a predefined structure and content to the information set that serves as a pattern for all companies. It would also include measures and discussion relevant to the specific perspective of the group.	1	2	3	4	5	dk
Maintain a facility on their website for free search (e.g. *via* provision of a search box), allowing users to retain control over the search and selection process (i.e. search software should support user-defined queries)	1	2	3	4	5	dk
To reduce unfair advantage, extend access to general company meetings with financial analysts/institutional shareholders by:						
placing records (*i.e.* presentation packs and slides) on website	1	2	3	4	5	dk
archiving an audio-visual record on website	1	2	3	4	5	dk
broadcasting live *via* satellite television channel or video webcast	1	2	3	4	5	dk
To reduce unfair advantage, extend access to one-to-one meetings by placing detailed minutes on website	1	2	3	4	5	dk
Teleconference (*i.e.* webcast) company AGMs to allow wider access	1	2	3	4	5	dk
Replace company AGMs by a facility for online questioning of management by users and conduct voting online	1	2	3	4	5	dk
Update business reporting information on websites periodically (*e.g.* quarterly or monthly), not continuously	1	2	3	4	5	dk
Distinguish clearly information that is continuously updated from more stable information that is updated only periodically	1	2	3	4	5	dk

Integration of information: navigation and search aids

Companies can be expected increasingly to design their business reporting packages for the Internet medium, rather than simply placing an exact reproduction of the printed Annual Report and Accounts on their website. Listed here are features relating to the navigation and search aids that have been adopted by leading edge companies or demonstration sites.

A5.   Please indicate how useful you think each of the following features would be in using an Internet-based business reporting package.

	Very useful	Useful	Fairly useful	Of little use	Not useful at all	Don't know
Business reporting information is clearly indexed on the home page (*e.g.* titled Investor Relations) and not buried (*e.g.* under company history)	1	2	3	4	5	dk
A hyperlinked site map or table of contents is available that shows all the major components in the business reporting package (hyperlinks allow the user to jump directly from one section to another, the link being activated by mouse-clicking on the source point)	1	2	3	4	5	dk
Hyperlinks exist between items in the financial statements and:						
• the relevant note to the accounts	1	2	3	4	5	dk
• the relevant section of the management discussion and analysis (known as the Operating and Financial Review (OFR) in the UK)	1	2	3	4	5	dk
• the five-year summary	1	2	3	4	5	dk
Hyperlinks exist between the:						
• individual notes to the accounts and the management discussion and analysis	1	2	3	4	5	dk
• management discussion and analysis and relevant forward-looking information	1	2	3	4	5	dk
• management discussion and analysis and relevant company background	1	2	3	4	5	dk
The facility to 'point and click' on financial items to get a time series graph of the item	1	2	3	4	5	dk
'Next' and 'previous' buttons at the bottom of each page	1	2	3	4	5	dk
Users can sign up for email alerts, to receive press releases and other updates *via* email or notification that new information is posted on the web	1	2	3	4	5	dk

Portability of information – file formats

A6.   Please indicate how useful you think each of the following formats and features would be in using an Internet-based business reporting package.

	Very useful	Useful	Fairly useful	Of little use	Not useful at all	Don't know
• Information is presented as a combination of text and graphics in a format designed for the Internet (*i.e.* Hypertext Mark-up Language (HTML)); documents can be viewed directly in the web browser, but can only be re-entered into other programs by hand	1	2	3	4	5	dk
• Information is presented as a Portable Document File (.pdf) that is produced by the Adobe Acrobat™ plug-in; data can only be transferred to other programs by cutting and pasting	1	2	3	4	5	dk
• Text information is presented as word-processed files in proprietary format (*e.g.* Microsoft Word™) which can be down-loaded and used with these applications	1	2	3	4	5	dk
• Financial statements are presented as spreadsheet files in proprietary format (*e.g.* Microsoft Excel™) which can be down-loaded and used with these applications	1	2	3	4	5	dk
• Information is structured so that applications can exchange data easily by using Extensible Mark-up Language (XML) [Note: a financial reporting version (XFRML) is being developed by the US professional accountancy body]	1	2	3	4	5	dk
• XFRML incorporates type tags that hook information together, allowing one company to be compared to others automatically	1	2	3	4	5	dk

REFERENCES

AICPA (1994), *Improving business reporting – a customer focus: meeting the information needs of investors and creditors,* Comprehensive Report of the Special Committee on Financial Reporting (The Jenkins Report), American Institute of Certified Public Accountants, New York, NY.

Ansoff I (1987), *Corporate strategy,* Penguin, Harmondsworth, Middlesex.

APB (2001), *The electronic publication of auditors' reports,* Bulletin 2001/1, Auditing Practices Board, London.

Arthur Andersen (2001), *It's raining news: a study of more frequent reporting by larger companies,* June, London.

Ashbaugh H, K M Johnston and T D Warfield (1999), 'Corporate reporting on the Internet', *Accounting Horizons,* Vol.13(3), September, pp241-257.

Beattie V A (2000), 'The future of corporate reporting: a review article', *Irish Accounting Review,* Vol.7(1), pp1-36.

Brennan N and D Hourigan (2000), 'Corporate reporting on the Internet by Irish companies', *The Irish Accounting Review,* Vol.7(1), pp37-68.

Bury L (1999), 'On line and on time', *Accountancy,* August, pp28-29.

Craven B M and C L Marston (1999), 'Financial reporting on the Internet by leading UK companies', *The European Accounting Review,* Vol.8(2), pp321-333.

Cyert R M and Y Ijiri (1974), 'Problems of implementing the Trueblood objectives report', *Journal of Accounting Research,* Supplement, pp29-45.

Deller D, M Stubenrath and C Weber (1999), 'A survey on the use of the Internet for investor relations in the USA, the UK and Germany', *The European Accounting Review,* Vol.8(2), pp351-364.

DTI (1998), *Modern company law for a competitive economy,* Consultation Paper, March, Department of Trade and Industry, London.

DTI (1999a), *Modern company law for a competitive economy: the strategic framework,* Consultation Document, February, Department of Trade and Industry, London.

DTI (1999b), *Company general meetings and shareholder communication,* Consultation Document, February, Department of Trade and Industry, London.

DTI (2000a), *Modern company law for a competitive economy: developing the framework,* Consultation Document, March, Company Law Review Steering Group. London.

DTI (2000b), *Modern company law for a competitive economy: completing the structure,* Consultation Document, November, Company Law Review Steering Group, London.

DTI (2001), *Modern company law for a competitive economy: final report, volume 1,* July, Company Law Review Steering Group, London.

Elliott R K (1992), 'The third wave breaks on the shores of accounting', *Accounting Horizons,* Vol.6(2), June, pp61-85.

Elliott R K (1994), 'Confronting the future: choices for the attest function', *Accounting Horizons,* Vol.8(3), September, pp106-124.

Elliott R K (2001), '21st century assurance', Address to the AAA Auditing Section Midyear Meeting, http://raw.rutgers.edu/raw/aaa/audit/ [visited 28th February 2001].

FASB (1998), http://www.rutgers.edu/Accounting/raw/fasb/fauxcom, Financial Accounting Standards Board, Norwark, CT [visited 24 August 1998].

FASB (2000), http://www.rutgers.edu/Accounting/raw/fasb/brrppg.html *Electronic distribution of business reporting information,* Financial Accounting Standards Board, Norwark, CT [visited 22 March 2000].

Financial Director (2000), 'Playing FTSE over the web', November, pp57-64.

Freeman R (1984), *Strategic management: a stakeholder approach,* Pitman, Boston.

Gowthorpe C and O Amat (1999), 'External reporting of accounting and financial information via the Internet in Spain', *The European Accounting Review,* Vol.8(2), pp365-371.

Hedlin P (1999), 'The Internet as a vehicle for investor information: the Swedish case', *The European Accounting Review,* Vol.8(2), pp373-381.

Hodge, F D (2001), 'Hyperlinking unaudited information to audited financial statements: effects on investor judgments', working paper, University of Washington.

Holland J (1998a), 'Private disclosure and financial reporting', *Accounting and Business Research,* Vol.28(4), Autumn, pp255-269.

Holland J (1998b), 'Private voluntary disclosure, financial intermediation and market efficiency', *Journal of Business Finance and Accounting,* Vol.25(1/2), January/March, pp29-68.

Hussey R, J Gulliford and A Lymer (1998), Corporate communication: financial reporting on the Internet, Deloitte and Touche, London.

Hussey R and M Sowinska (1999), 'The risks of financial reports on the Internet', *Accounting & Business,* March, pp18-19.

IASC (1999), *Business reporting on the Internet,* Discussion Paper prepared by Lymer A, R Debreceny,G L Gray and A Rahman, November, International Accounting Standards Committee, London.

ICAS (1999), *Business reporting: the inevitable change?,* Beattie V (ed.), Institute of Chartered Accountants of Scotland, Edinburgh.

ICAEW (1998), *The 21st century annual report,* Papers from a conference held on the 11th September, Institute of Chartered Accountants in England and Wales, London.

Investor Relations Society (1998), *Annual reports and the Internet,* Investor Relations Society, London.

Louwers T J, W R Pasewark and E W Typpo (1996), 'The Internet: changing the way corporations tell their story', *CPA Journal,* Vol.66(11), pp 24-28.

Lymer A and A Tallberg (1997), 'Corporate reporting and the Internet: a survey and commentary on the use of the WWW in corporate reporting in the UK and Finland', paper presented at the 20th Annual Congress of the European Accounting Association, Graz, Austria, April http://www.summa.org.uk/SUMMA/corp/papers/papers.html [visited 30 October 1998].

Marston C and C Y Leow (1998), 'Financial reporting on the Internet by leading UK companies', EAA conference paper, available at http://www.summa.org.uk/SUMMA/corp/papers/marston/marston.html

McCausland R (2000), 'Speaking XBRL: the new talk of accounting', *Accounting Technology,* Vol.16(5), pp52-56. Available from http://www.electronicaccountant.com

Nordberg D (1999), 'Shareholder communication: the next wave', Centre for Business Performance, Institute of Chartered Accountants in England and Wales, London.

Petravick S and J W Gillett (1998), 'Distributing earnings reports on the Internet', *Management Accounting* (USA), Vol.80(4), pp54-56.

Pirchegger B and A Wagenhofer (1999), 'Financial information on the Internet: a survey of the homepages of Austrian companies', *The European Accounting Review,* Vol.8(2), pp383-395.

PricewaterhouseCoopers (2000), *ValueReporting™ Forecast: 2001: trends in corporate reporting,* PricewaterhouseCoopers.

ProShare (1999), *Managing relationships with private investors,* ProShare, London.

Richardson V J and Scholz S (2000), 'Corporate reporting and the Internet: vision, reality, and intervening obstacles', *Pacific Accounting Review,* Vol.11(2), pp153-159.

Romain G (2000), 'Legislation in moderation', *Accountancy,* December, p92.

RSA (1995), *Tomorrow's company: the role of business in a changing world,* Royal Society of Arts, London.

RSA (1998), *Sooner, sharper, simpler: a lean vision of an inclusive annual report,* Royal Society of Arts, London.

Taylor S (1998), *Web sites – a missed opportunity?,* Business Briefing, Institute of Chartered Accountants in England and Wales, London.

Thompson G (1996), 'Communications assets in the information age: the impact of technology on corporate communications', *Corporate Communications: An International Journal,* Vol.1(3), pp8-10.

Trites G (1999a), *The impact of technology on financial and business reporting,* Canadian Institute of Chartered Accountants, Toronto.

Trites G (1999b), 'Democratising disclosure', *CA Magazine* (Canadian), October, p47.

Wallman S M H (1995), 'The future of accounting and disclosure in an evolving world: the need for dramatic change', *Accounting Horizons,* Vol.9(3), September, pp81-91.

Wallman S M H (1997), 'The future of accounting and financial reporting, part IV: "access" accounting', *Accounting Horizons,* Vol.11(2), June, pp103-116.

Watts R L and J L Zimmerman (1986), *Positive accounting theory,* Prentice-Hall International, Englewood Cliffs, NJ.

XBRL (2000), http://www.xfrml.org and related sites [visited 5 April 2000 and 1 February 2001].

Xiao, Z, M Jones and A Lymer (2000), 'Immediate trends in Internet reporting', BAA Conference paper.